History: A Very Short Introduction

'A stimulating and provocative introduction to one of collective humanity's most important quests – understanding the past and its relation to the present. A vivid mix of telling examples and clear-cut analysis.'
David Lowenthal, University College, London

'This is an extremely engaging book, lively, enthusiastic and highly readable, which presents some of the fundamental problems of historical writing in a lucid and accessible manner. As an invitation to the study of history it should be difficult to resist.'
Peter Burke, Emmanuel College, Cambridge

'A few millennia of events, millions of manuscripts tucked away, uncountable lives passed, endless stories to tell. History: where to begin? John Arnold's *History: A Very Short Introduction* is an excellent very short answer. Lucid and thoughtfully written, it will inspire confidence in students who wish to seek their own historical answers.'
Dorothy Porter, Birkbeck College, London

'intriguing and original in its discussion of why history matters and what are the problems inherent in studying it. The book is admirable in being discursive and thought-provoking'
Paul Freedman, Yale University

Very Short Introductions available now:

ANCIENT PHILOSOPHY
  Julia Annas
THE ANGLO-SAXON AGE
  John Blair
ANIMAL RIGHTS
  David DeGrazia
ARCHAEOLOGY   Paul Bahn
ARISTOTLE   Jonathan Barnes
AUGUSTINE   Henry Chadwick
BARTHES   Jonathan Culler
THE BIBLE   John Riches
BUDDHA   Michael Carrithers
BUDDHISM   Damien Keown
CLASSICS   Mary Beard and
  John Henderson
CLAUSEWITZ   Michael Howard
CONTINENTAL PHILOSOPHY
  Simon Critchley
COSMOLOGY   Peter Coles
DARWIN   Jonathan Howard
DESCARTES   Tom Sorell
DRUGS   Leslie Iversen
EIGHTEENTH-CENTURY
  BRITAIN   Paul Langford
THE EUROPEAN UNION
  John Pinder
THE FRENCH REVOLUTION
  William Doyle
FREUD   Anthony Storr
GALILEO   Stillman Drake
GANDHI   Bhikhu Parekh
HEGEL   Peter Singer
HEIDEGGER   Michael Inwood
HINDUISM   Kim Knott
HISTORY   John H. Arnold
HOBBES   Richard Tuck
HUME   A. J. Ayer
INDIAN PHILOSOPHY
  Sue Hamilton
INTELLIGENCE   Ian J. Deary
ISLAM   Malise Ruthven
JUDAISM   Norman Solomon
JUNG   Anthony Stevens

KANT   Roger Scruton
KIERKEGAARD   Patrick Gardiner
THE KORAN   Michael Cook
LITERARY THEORY
  Jonathan Culler
LOGIC   Graham Priest
MACHIAVELLI   Quentin Skinner
MARX   Peter Singer
MEDIEVAL BRITAIN
  John Gillingham and
  Ralph A. Griffiths
MUSIC   Nicholas Cook
NIETZSCHE   Michael Tanner
NINETEENTH-CENTURY
  BRITAIN   Christopher Harvie and
  H. C. G. Matthew
PAUL   E. P. Sanders
PHILOSOPHY   Edward Craig
POLITICS   Kenneth Minogue
PSYCHOLOGY   Gillian Butler and
  Freda McManus
ROMAN BRITAIN
  Peter Salway
ROUSSEAU   Robert Wokler
RUSSELL   A. C. Grayling
RUSSIAN LITERATURE
  Catriona Kelly
THE RUSSIAN REVOLUTION
  S. A. Smith
SCHOPENHAUER
  Christopher Janaway
SHAKESPEARE   Germaine Greer
SOCIAL AND CULTURAL
  ANTHROPOLOGY
  John Monaghan and Peter Just
SOCIOLOGY   Steve Bruce
SOCRATES   C. C. W. Taylor
STUART BRITAIN   John Morrill
THEOLOGY   David F. Ford
THE TUDORS   John Guy
TWENTIETH-CENTURY
  BRITAIN   Kenneth O. Morgan
WITTGENSTEIN   A. C. Grayling

For more information visit our web site
www.oup.co.uk/vsi

John H. Arnold

HISTORY

A Very Short Introduction

OXFORD
UNIVERSITY PRESS

OXFORD
UNIVERSITY PRESS

Great Clarendon Street, Oxford OX2 6DP

Oxford University Press is a department of the University of Oxford.
It furthers the University's objective of excellence in research, scholarship,
and education by publishing worldwide in

Oxford New York

Athens Auckland Bangkok Bogotá Buenos Aires Calcutta
Cape Town Chennai Dar es Salaam Delhi Florence Hong Kong Istanbul
Karachi Kuala Lumpur Madrid Melbourne Mexico City Mumbai
Nairobi Paris São Paulo Shanghai Singapore Taipei Tokyo Toronto Warsaw

with associated companies in Berlin Ibadan

Oxford is a registered trade mark of Oxford University Press
in the UK and in certain other countries

Published in the United States
by Oxford University Press Inc., New York

© John H. Arnold 2000

The moral rights of the author have been asserted
Database right Oxford University Press (maker)

First published as an Oxford University Press paperback 2000

British Library Cataloguing in Publication Data

Data available

Library of Congress Cataloging in Publication Data

Data available

ISBN 0–19–285352–X

7 9 10 8

Typeset by RefineCatch Ltd, Bungay, Suffolk
Printed in Spain by Book Print S. L.

For Mum, Dad, Ruth, and Victoria

Preface and acknowledgements

There are perhaps three kinds of books one can write on the subject of 'history' in general. One is a 'how-to' guide to practice. Another is a philosophical investigation into theories of knowledge. The third is a polemic supporting a particular approach. This book is an introduction to history, and cannot claim to be fully any of these things, although it takes a little from each. Overall, however, it is intended as a work of *enthusiasm*. What is written here presents my views on what history is, how it is researched, and what it is for. I have, however, always tried to indicate that there are other paths to follow, other arguments to discover; and I hope that the reader might be tempted into some further exploration.

The book is loosely arranged into three sections. The first three chapters aim to raise certain questions, engage the reader's interest, and describe (in brief terms) what history has been in the past. Chapters 4 and 5 attempt to show how one might set about 'doing' history, first by working with sources and secondly by thinking about interpretations. The final chapters present some thoughts on the status and meaning of history and truth, and why history matters.

The chapters here have had many readers prior to their final versions, and I have incurred great debts towards a number of people who have set me straight on various topics. In particular, I must thank Barbara

MacAllan, an expert on East Anglian migration to the New World, who first set me on the trail of George Burdett. Without her extreme generosity Chapter 4 would not have been written. Any remaining foolishness, on this or any other area, is entirely my own property. Those others exculpated of guilt, but deserving of gratitude, include the following: Edward Acton, Katherine Benson, Peter Biller, Stephen Church, Shelley Cox, Simon Crabtree, Richard Crockett, Geoff Cubitt, Simon Ditchfield, Victoria Howell, Chris Humphrey, Mark Knights, Peter Martin, Simon Middleton, George Miller, Carol Rawcliffe, Andy Wood, and a host of anonymous readers at OUP. For what they have taught me about history, I have to thank the staff and students at the Department of History and the Centre for Medieval Studies at the University of York, and the schools of History, and of English and American Studies, at the University of East Anglia. Lastly, I have the longest debt to my father, who is always willing to argue about history and to tell me why I'm wrong.

Contents

List of Illustrations

Chapter 1
Questions about murder and history

Here is a true story. In 1301 Guilhem de Rodes hurried down from his Pyrenean village of Tarascon to the town of Pamiers, in the south of France. He was on his way to visit his brother Raimond, who was a monk in the Dominican monastery there. The journey was a good thirty kilometres along the gorge of the river Ariège, and it would take Guilhem at least a day to reach his destination, travelling as he was on foot. But the reason for his trip was urgent: his brother had sent him a letter warning that both of them were in great danger. He had to come at once.

When he reached the monastery at Pamiers, his brother had frightening news. Raimond told him that a certain *beguin* (a kind of quasi-monk, who did not belong to any official religious order) had recently visited the monastery. He was called Guilhem Déjean, and he posed a real threat to the brothers. Déjean had apparently offered to help the Dominicans catch two heretics – Pierre and Guilhem Autier – who were based in the Pyrenean village of Montaillou. He knew about the heretics because a man, who had given him shelter for the night, up in the mountain villages, had innocently offered to introduce Déjean to them, thinking he might join their faith. Déjean had met the Autiers, and gained their trust; now he could betray them.

But what really terrified Raimond was that Déjean had also claimed that the heretics had a spy within the monastery. This spy, the *beguin* said, was linked to the heretics through his brother, a member of the laity, and a friend of the Autiers. The brother was Guilhem de Rodes; the alleged spy was Raimond de Rodes. 'Is this true?' demanded the frightened Raimond. 'Have you had contact with the heretics?'. 'No', replied Guilhem de Rodes. 'The *beguin* is a liar'.

This was itself a lie. Guilhem de Rodes had first met the heretics in the spring of 1298. He had listened to their preaching, had given them food and shelter, and was in fact related to them: they were his uncles. The Autiers had recently returned from Lombardy, having previously been notaries working for the small villages and towns around the Ariège river. In Lombardy they had converted to the Cathar faith, which had been dominant in southern France during the thirteenth century, but had died out in more recent years under the attentions of the inquisitors. Pierre and Guilhem Autier were to start a revival.

Catharism was a Christian heresy. Those who held the Cathar faith called themselves 'Good Christians' and believed that they were the true inheritors of the mission of the apostles. They also believed that there were two Gods: a Good God, who created the spirit, and a Bad God who created all corporeal matter. This 'dualist' belief was antithetical to Roman Catholic orthodoxy; and in any case, the Cathars believed that the Roman Catholic Church was corrupt – 'the Whore of Babylon' they called it. In the early thirteenth century there were several thousand Cathars, and many more believers, in the south of France. By the early fourteenth century, however, only fourteen Cathars survived, largely hidden in the Pyrenean villages. Nonetheless, such beliefs were not tolerated by the orthodox powers. Hence the eagerness of the Dominicans at Pamiers to take the opportunity to capture the Autiers. Hence too the danger that Guilhem Déjean posed to the de Rodes brothers.

Guilhem de Rodes left his brother and returned home to the Pyrenees.

He travelled to the village of Ax (another thirty kilometres from Tarascon) to warn Raimond Autier (brother of the heretics) about Déjean. Once back in his home village, he also warned a man called Guilhem de Area, who lived in the neighbouring settlement of Quié. We do not know if he intended thus to set in motion the events that subsequently transpired.

Guilhem de Area was a great supporter of the Cathars. He immediately sought out the *beguin* Déjean, and asked him if he was looking for the Autiers. 'Yes', replied Déjean; so Guilhem de Area offered to lead him to them. Pleased, and unsuspecting, the *beguin* agreed. They travelled together to the village of Larnat, deeper into the mountains.

Guilhem de Rodes heard that later the same night, as the *beguin* reached the bridge outside Larnat, two men appeared: Philippe de Larnat and Pierre de Area (Guilhem de Area's brother). And this is what happened:

> Immediately they grabbed him [Déjean] and struck him so that he had not the strength to cry out. They took him to the mountains around Larnat, and there they asked him if it was true that he wanted to capture the heretics. He admitted that it was; and instantly Philippe and Pierre threw him off a great cliff, into a crevasse.

The murder remained a secret for many years. Guilhem de Rodes, Raimond de Rodes, and the Autiers were safe for the time being.

What are we to make of this long-forgotten murder? It was recorded in the registers of inquisition in the year 1308, when Guilhem de Rodes confessed what he knew about heresy and heretics. It was retold by three other witnesses. For his contact with the Cathars, Guilhem was sentenced to prison, along with sixty other people. It survives for us as a small, dark, fascinating vignette from the fourteenth century. This then is 'history': a true story of something that happened long ago, retold in

3

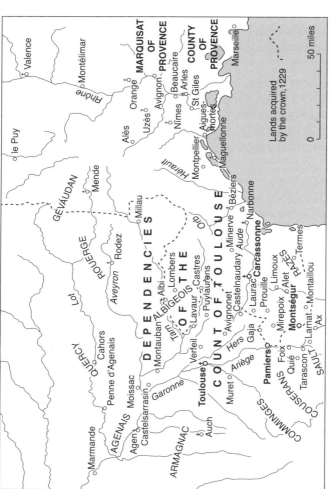

1. Towns and villages in Languedoc (southwestern France) in the middle ages. Guilhem Déjean's corpse presumably lies south of Larnat.

the present. The past is brought to life once more, and the unequal contact between then and now has been re-established. Is the historian thus acquitted of his or her task, and this short introduction to History now concluded?

Let us not end our journey quite so soon. There are lingering questions about the murder of Guilhem Déjean, and questions waiting to be asked about history in general. The process of writing history ('historiography') is full of questions, as this book will show. We can use this first chapter to begin to examine these questions, some of which may have already sprung to mind. In many ways, history both begins and ends with questions; which is to say that it never really ends, but is a *process*.

Language can be confusing. 'History' often refers to both the past itself, and to what historians write about the past. 'Histori-ography' can mean either the process of writing history, or the study of that process. In this book, I use 'historiography' to mean the process of writing history; and 'history' to mean the end product of that process. As we will see, this book argues that there is an essential difference between 'history' (as I am using it) and 'the past'.

How, then, did the above story arrive upon these pages? There are several different answers here. We can begin with the simplest. Guilhem de Rodes appeared before an inquisitor called Geoffroi d'Ablis on four occasions in 1308. D'Ablis had come to investigate heresy in the Pyrenees on the authority of the Pope. He was allowed to command anyone and everyone to appear before him to answer questions relating to the orthodox faith, and to demand that they confess not only their own actions but also those of others, both living and dead. Having heard their confessions, the inquisitor could impose a penance or punishment, which ranged from wearing yellow crosses to indicate that a witness had been guilty of heretical activities, to being burned alive at the stake.

The investigation that caught up Guilhem de Rodes was initially prompted by Géraud de Rodes, another brother of Guilhem's, who came spontaneously to the inquisitor and named many people for their involvement in Catharism. His confession, Guilhem's confession, and those of at least fifteen others, were recorded in the inquisitorial registers. The witnesses responded to set questions asked by d'Ablis, and supplied some material of their own; their answers were recorded by the inquisitor's scribes, and stored for safe keeping and further use. Some of these registers have survived, so their fourteenth-century speech is still with us. This particular register has been edited and printed by a modern historian. I have used some of the material to bring you the story of Guilhem Déjean.

The questions, however, do not end there. In a later chapter I shall say more about evidence, its uses, and its problems. For now, look back at the story. I hope that it engaged your attention; I chose it because it certainly engaged mine. It grabs us, perhaps, because it is a murder, and we are familiar with the guilty pleasure of sharing horror stories. It is also clearly a 'story' in that it has a beginning, middle, and end, which might make it more 'satisfying'. It may interest and surprise us, if we were not previously aware that medieval people got up to such activities. The people in the story were not kings or princes or saints or famous writers, they were everyday people. We may therefore simply be diverted to discover that we know anything about them at all!

Perhaps the story also interests us because of what is strange about it. It has been suggested (by the writer L. P. Hartley) that 'the past is a foreign country; they do things differently there'. Douglas Adams, the science-fiction author, posits an opposite case: the past is truly a foreign country, they do things just *like* us. Somewhere between these two

6

propositions is the elusive element that attracts us to the past, and prompts us to study history. The story told above speaks to both statements. We understand and relate to sending letters, visiting relatives, journeys from our hometown. We know about fear of persecution and we know about murder, even if we have not experienced them at first hand. If I had translated the participants' names into your vernacular language ('Guilhem' would become 'William' in English) then they might seem even closer to us. The names I have used are from Occitan, the language of that time and period. Here in fact I have cheated slightly; the records are in Latin, so perhaps I should have employed that tongue, which uses the version *Guillelmus*.

But the names are strange to us in a different way. It seems odd to find so many people all called Guilhem; and we do not often use our place of birth to render our surnames ('de Rodes' meaning 'of the place called Rodes'). We know about religion, but we are probably unfamiliar with the concept of heresy, the workings of inquisition, and the belief in two Gods. Do we see this as a bizarre 'superstition'? Or as no stranger an idea than the Son of God descending to Earth, dying on the cross and then being resurrected? 'Heresy' can only exist where there is an 'orthodoxy' to define it: both medieval Catholics and medieval Cathars laid claim to being 'true' Christians. Whatever our current philosophies and religious beliefs, can we lay claim to a real connection with either group?

If we read more of the records, other elements of difference would strike us too. Although Guilhem de Rodes and his brother were clearly able to read and write (they communicated by letter) they are quite unusual in this: most people at that time would not have had as much access to literacy. Indeed, the concept of 'literacy' was rather different in the fourteenth century: if you were described as *litteratus* ('literate') this meant that you could read and write *Latin* and knew how to interpret scripture. Facility in vernacular languages did not count as 'literacy', no matter how useful that ability was. Reading and writing

Occitan (or German, French, English, and so on) would still label you *illiteratus* ('illiterate'). These elements of familiarity and strangeness may prompt further questions.

Guilhem Déjean's murder was not the only event recorded in the inquisition registers. It was obviously not the only event to take place during 1301 in the Pyrenees, in southern France, in Europe, or the world in general. Historians cannot tell *every* story from the past, only some of them. There are gaps in the material that exists (some of the pages of d'Ablis's register are missing) and there are areas for which no evidence survives. But even with the evidence we do have, there are many more things that *could* be said than we have space to discuss. Historians inevitably decide which things can or should be said. So 'history' (the true stories historians tell about the past) is made up only of those things which have caught our attention, that we have decided to repeat for modern ears. As we will see in a later chapter, the grounds on which historians have selected their true stories have changed over the years.

Having picked Déjean's murder as a story we wish to repeat, we also need to decide how it will play a part in a larger picture. It would be unusual for a modern historian simply to present a vignette such as the one above, and to say nothing more. In the late nineteenth and early twentieth centuries some historians did work in this way, collecting and translating interesting pieces of evidence they thought might appeal to a wider readership. Such books are useful treasure troves, and have led to detailed work by other historians. They can be a pleasure to read, infecting readers with their enthusiasm for the past. But for most modern historians, this is not enough. We need to *interpret* the past, not simply present it. Finding a larger context for the story is an attempt to say not just 'what happened' but what it meant.

Into what larger pictures can we fit the story of Déjean's murder? There are several possibilities. Most obviously, the account fits into a wider history of inquisition and heresy. It tells us about people involved with

8

2. St Dominic combats Cathar heretics (depicted on the right). Books were thrown onto the fire: the heretical works burned, but the orthodox texts rose miraculously into the air. In reality, Dominic was not an inquisitor (although later members of his order were); but burning by fire remained the final punishment for unrepentant heretics. (Pedro Berruguete, late fifteenth century)

the Cathar faith, their actions and beliefs. It tells us of the history of Catharism itself: reading the d'Ablis register, we discover something about how many people were converted by the Autier heretics. We could note that people in the evidence do not talk of 'The Inquisition' but only of 'inquisitors'. This is because 'The Inquisition' did not exist as a formal institution in this period; there were only individual inquisitors (such as Geoffroi d'Ablis) who had particular jobs to do (in his case, to investigate heresy in the Pyrenean villages). 'Inquisition' meant the legal process that d'Ablis and others carried out. It had been established as a method of combating heresy in the early years of the thirteenth century. His register also shows us how the process of inquisition – how it set about investigating and recording heresy – had changed since that time. If we compared Guilhem de Rodes's confession to one made in the 1240s, we would find that Guilhem was encouraged to talk at much greater length and in much more detail than witnesses from the earlier years of inquisition. This was because the threat posed by heresy had changed, and the remit of the inquisitors was changing with it.

Alternatively, we could fit Déjean's murder into a history of crime. There are other accounts of murders in the Middle Ages, some of them quite famous. We could contrast this story with the murder of Thomas Becket in 1170, or the execution of William Wallace in 1304, or the alleged crimes of Richard III of England. Or we could concentrate upon crimes within the lower orders of society, using other kinds of court records to find them, and talk about the preponderance of violence in the Middle Ages, the methods used, the investigations and punishments, and the motives of the criminals. Yet again, the story could play a part in the history of Languedoc. 'Languedoc' means 'the tongue (or language) of Oc', and was the name given to this area of southern France, because its inhabitants used the word 'oc' to mean 'yes', rather than 'oui' which was used in the north. Because of the presence of heresy in Languedoc, the Pope had ordered a crusade against the land in the early thirteenth century. Previously, Languedoc had been almost a separate country, feeling more kinship with Catalonia than with the area around Paris.

This crusade against heresy resulted in the north of France taking political control of the south. It was a long while before Languedoc settled down under its new political masters, and in some ways the south of France still sees itself as very different from the Parisian north. The defence of Catharism (including, perhaps, Déjean's murder) was bound up in the history of French politics.

Finally, we could ignore the narrative of the story, and concentrate on its small details. I mentioned the matter of literacy above; this is a useful nugget for a historian interested in levels of learning amongst the laity. Déjean was attacked on a bridge outside Larnat; reading further records from the register we discover that there was a bridge outside Tarascon too, and other villages also. This tells us something about the geography of the land. Guilhem de Rodes mentions elsewhere in his confession that he once hid the heretics in 'a place under the floor used as a grain store'. Another time the heretics stayed in a hut that Guilhem owned in a field near Tarascon. In this way we can find out things about agriculture and architecture. Elsewhere Guilhem says that he travelled to the village of Ax on business; and that once he was away doing military training with the Count of Foix. We know, then, more about Guilhem's activities, and hence by extension, other people of his social class. Guilhem was often asked to give a date to the events he confessed. He usually referred to a saint's day, saying for example 'it was fifteen days after the feast of St John the Baptist' (some time in June). This gives us a picture of how Guilhem perceived the passage of time, and the importance of saints even to someone with heretical sympathies. If we mined the other inquisition records for further nuggets, we might amass a useful hoard of such information. There is a whole world surrounding Guilhem's confession; a world which he took largely for granted, which is revealed to us in tantalizing shards and fragments.

These are some of the pictures that occur to me as the possible contexts for the story of Déjean's murder. Other readers will think of other things. As we will see further on, historians in other times would have interpreted this story differently. Some would not have thought it important or intriguing at all. These choices are not just to do with chance or cleverness, but with what *interests* us. As historians, we are caught up in our own bundles of interests, morals, ethics, philosophies, ideas on how the world works, and why people do the things they do. The evidence of the records presents us with pictures and puzzles; challenges, in fact. Guilhem de Rodes does not explain every detail of his story. For example, the evidence does not tell us why no-one at the monastery questioned his brother; nor what Guilhem Déjean's motives were exactly (was he devoutly orthodox or hoping to gain the Dominicans' approval?); nor precisely what prompted Guilhem de Area and his accomplices to pitch Déjean into his dark and rocky grave (were they protecting the Autiers, or protecting themselves?) I have ideas about these things, but they are *my* ideas. Later in this book we shall talk more about how historians fill in these blanks, and the art of good guessing.

'Guessing' suggests a degree of uncertainty about the historiographical process. It might even suggest that at times historians get things wrong. They do, of course: historians, like everyone else, can misread, misremember, misinterpret, or misunderstand things. But in a wider sense, historians *always* get things 'wrong'. We do this first because we cannot ever get it *totally* 'right'. Every historical account has gaps, problems, contradictions, areas of uncertainty. We also get it 'wrong' because we cannot always agree with each other; we need to get it 'wrong' in our own ways (although, as we shall see, we sometimes form different groups in how we interpret things). However, whilst getting it wrong, historians always *attempt* to get it 'right'. We try to stick to what we think the evidence actually says, to search out all the available material, to understand fully what is happening, and we never fabricate 'the facts'. Historians sometimes like to define their work against that of literature. An author of fiction can invent people, places, and happenings, whereas a historian is bound by what the evidence will support. This comparison might make history seem somewhat dry and unimaginative. However, as we have seen and will further explore, history also involves imagination, in dealing with that evidence, presenting it, and explaining it. For every historian, what is at stake is what actually happened – and what it might *mean*. There is an excitement to these precarious attempts to grasp the 'truth', a truth that might at any point be revealed as illusory.

These doubts are necessary for 'history' to exist. If the past came without gaps and problems, there would be no task for the historian to complete. And if the evidence that existed always spoke plainly, truthfully, and clearly to us, not only would historians have no work to do, we would have no opportunity to argue with each other. History is above all else an *argument*. It is an argument between different historians; and, perhaps, an argument between the past and the present, an argument between what actually happened, and what is going to happen next. Arguments are important; they create the possibility of changing things.

It is for these reasons that throughout this chapter and this book I have used the term 'true stories' to talk about history. There is a necessary tension here: history is 'true' in that it must agree with the evidence, the facts that it calls upon; or else, it must show why those 'facts' are wrong, and need reworking. At the same time, it is a 'story', in that it is an *interpretation*, placing those 'facts' within a wider context or narrative. Historians tell stories, in the sense that they are out to persuade you (and themselves) of something. Their methods of persuasion depend in part upon the 'truth' – not making things up, not presenting matters as other than they are – but also in creating an interesting, coherent and useful narrative about the past. The past itself is not a narrative. In its entirety, it is as chaotic, uncoordinated, and complex as life. History is about making sense of that mess, finding or creating patterns and meanings and stories from the maelstrom.

We have begun with a series of questions, and I have presented some propositions: that history is a process, an argument, and is composed of true stories about the past. These things we explore more fully in the rest of the book. But one last thing: thinking about history (as we are doing here) presents us with both opportunities and dangers. It allows us to reflect upon our relationship to the past, to look at the kinds of stories we have chosen to tell about the past, the ways in which we have come to those stories, and the *effects* of telling those stories. When the past re-enters the present, it becomes a powerful place. Part of thinking about 'history' is to think about what – or who – history is *for*. To begin this enquiry, we might find it useful to look backwards, to attempt to understand what 'history' has been in the past.

Chapter 2

From the tails of dolphins to the tower of politics

In the sixth century BC, a Babylonian king named Nabonidus conducted a search – perhaps we could say an early archaeological dig – for an ancient temple, an *E-babbar*. He found it, and he wrote about his discovery:

> I read there the inscription of the ancient king Hammurabi, who had built for Shamash, seven hundred years before Burnaburiash, the *E-babbar* on the ancient *temenos* and I understood its meaning. I adored with trembling . . .

The king Burnaburiash had lived in the fourteenth century BC, and the temple of the god Shamash found by Nabonidus was, in turn, seven hundred years older; that is, the temple was two millennia older than Nabonidus. Such incredible gaps of time start to make Nabonidus seem somewhat closer to ourselves. If we see his discovery and writing as the beginning of our story, as the first bit of 'history' that we know about, the sense of closeness might be strengthened by his role as an 'origin' in the narrative of this chapter. Such a sense of connection is useful, but can cause us problems: Nabonidus was interested in finding the *E-babbar* because of the connection it allowed him with his own royal tradition, and the power and authority implied by that connection. How he understood his discovery, and his motives for recording it, are not necessarily the same as our own interest in history.

Can we look back in this way to the beginning of 'history' as an activity? The question is complex, and in asking it we are, of course, engaged in our own, contemporary, historical enquiry. We can look back to 'historicize' history itself; that is, to see what its roots are, where it comes from, how it has changed, and what it has been used for in different times and places. Our focus, here in this brief account, has to be upon the present: to use past historiography as a comparison to what we do now, and as a reminder that if history, as a subject, has changed over time, it may yet change again. Consequently, there will be large gaps in the story that follows. However, part of what I wish to show is that *all* history in some ways wishes to say something about its own present time.

Let us move forward a century to the first Greek historian. Herodotus (484–425 BC) wrote about the historical causes of the conflicts between the Greeks and the Persians, a topic that Homer had previously dealt with in his poetry. Herodotus begins his histories by discussing the older stories of why the two peoples came to blows. He recounts the Persian version of events: that Phoenicians had kidnapped Io, daughter of the Greek king; that the Greeks had kidnapped Europa, daughter of the Phoenician king, and then Medea, another royal daughter; and that Paris, son of a Phoenician ruler called Priam, was inspired by these stories to kidnap Helen, to make her his wife. In Phoenician eyes, none of this was terribly important: kidnapping women was bad, but not the sort of thing to get very upset about, 'for it is obvious that that no young woman allows herself to be abducted if she does not wish to be'. The Greeks, however, over-reacted: they raised a great army to rescue Helen of Troy, and destroyed the empire of Priam. All this was caused by the tit-for-tat abduction of women. The Phoenician historians, however, say that even this account is untrue: Io (the first woman mentioned) was not taken by force, but had become pregnant by the captain of a Phoenician ship, and had chosen to go back with him rather than shame her parents.

Herodotus writes:

> So much for what Persians and Phoenicians say; and I have no intention
> of passing judgement on its truth or falsity. I prefer to rely on my own
> knowledge, and to point out who it was in actual fact that first injured
> the Greeks; then I will proceed with my history, telling the story as I go
> along of small cities no less than great. Most of those which were great
> once are small today; and those which in my own lifetime have grown
> to greatness, were small enough in the old days. It makes no odds
> whether the cities I shall write of are big or little – for in this world
> nobody remains prosperous for long.

In rejecting the Persian legends, Herodotus chooses to rely upon 'the
facts' rather than spurious beliefs. Later in his book, he uses an account
from oral history to show that Helen and Paris never actually reached
Troy, but were detained in Egypt; and analyses a few passages from
Homer to argue that the great poet actually knew about this, but chose
to follow a different, fictional, story. Whether or not we believe
Herodotus' new account of Helen's history, his attempt to use evidence
to distinguish a fictional story from a true, historical account makes him
look much like a twentieth-century historian. The fact that his *Histories*
are not linked simply to his personal circumstances (like Nabonidus and
the *E-babbar*) but address a wider audience and have a wider purpose
(to record and explain the past) also suggest that Herodotus is the
founder of history as we know it today. Indeed, he is sometimes labelled
the 'Father of History'.

But again we must be careful here. Although parts of Herodotus may
seem familiar and 'modern', other parts do not. Much of the history he
tells concerns tales we would find unbelievable: of Arion who rode on
the tail of a dolphin; of Adrastus who accidentally killed first his father,
was given shelter by the ruler Croesus, and then accidentally killed
Croesus' son too; and of the Delphic oracle, whose predictions
punctuate the story, and always come true. These stories, and others,

are mixed up with what we would recognize as a more 'factual' political history of how the Greeks and Persians went to war. Herodotus is always happy to diverge from his account of political events to tell us about the local customs of a people, the weird and wonderful animals in different areas, and any fabulous story that had caught his interest. Herodotus is therefore also known as the 'Father of Lies'. But Herodotus himself would not have seen any difference between these elements: indeed, he often takes pains to state that what he is saying can be believed because of the witnesses who confirm it.

There are other reasons to see Herodotus as different from us. For one thing, it is unlikely that Herodotus saw his writing of a 'history' as being essentially different from other kinds of writing. The Greek word which has become 'history' originally meant 'to inquire', and more specifically indicated a person who was able to choose wisely between conflicting accounts. Applying this to writing about the past, it largely meant that the work was neither poetic nor philosophical; and hence, for the Greeks, rather less important. It is not at all clear that it occupied a particular genre called 'History'; it is more likely that it was seen as one part of a larger body of 'non-philosophical' writing. Also, although Herodotus' reason for writing is more like our own than that of Nabonidus, it is still somewhat different. Herodotus uses the past to provide illustrations of situations and characters for use in his present time. He does this because he sees time as circular: history revolving around and around, with the same themes and problems arising again and again. The events that take place in his *Histories* are often caused by flaws in character, but behind these flaws lies the circular wheel of fate, which (as he says above) raises up and pulls down cities and people in equal measure. For example, he tells of Croesus who, despite being warned in a dream, could not prevent the death of his son (the one accidentally killed by Adrastus); and who went on to lose his entire empire, all through hubris (the pride in one's achievements that provokes the ire of the gods). Some twentieth-century historians may

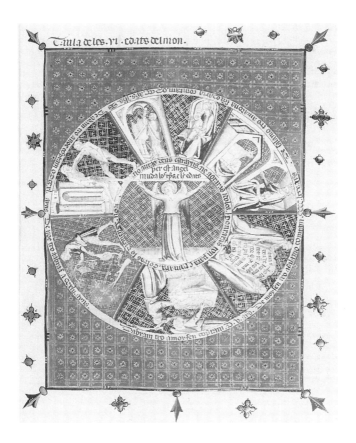

3. Augustine's Six Ages of Man (and therefore history) are represented here in a circle, reminiscent of the wheel of fate depicted in Fig. 4. The seventh age yet to come would be the apocalypse.

believe that certain themes recur in history; but none I think believes that the wheel of fate governs causality.

This concept of time arguably changed when Christianity produced its first historians. Christian belief did not depend upon the wheel of fate; instead it saw the world moving inexorably between two fixed points, the Creation and the Apocalypse. Drawing on the Old Testament, early Christian historians also posited Seven Ages of mankind. By the time they were writing, the first five ages had already gone, and humanity had entered the sixth age, the period from the birth of Christ to his

4. Wheel of Fortune, by William de Brailes (1235)

Second Coming. All that lay ahead was the seventh age, the period of the Apocalypse and the end of history. This framework suggested a rather different idea about what history might mean, and how one should approach it.

However, one should not draw too sharp a divide between the classical period and the early Christian era: the image of the wheel of fate did in fact continue within Christian culture, and the concept of the Seven Ages did not dictate all that was written within Christian history. What did effect a change in historiography, however, was a new and pressing *purpose* to history. Eusebius's *Ecclesiastical History* (written c.325 AD) aims to persuade Christian and pagan audiences that Christianity was more ancient, more rational, more moral, and more valid than pagan religion. The early Christians wrote history as a *polemical* account of the past. They did this because they were, in those first few centuries, a beleaguered people who had to defend a faith that was being persecuted by the Roman authorities. Providing a history for their faith (and against other faiths) was an attempt to gain authority. Augustine of Hippo, in the *City of God* (written c.426), tried to conjoin the historical struggles of his church with the eternal battle between spirituality and wickedness. This was a mixture of theology and history on a grand scale, but was too long and too complex to have much immediate influence. However, Augustine's pupil Orosius wrote a simplified and more polemical version, *History against the pagans*, which was much more popular.

Eusebius and Orosius set about creating authoritative histories by copying out original documents that aided their case, by insisting on the historical accuracy of Scripture, and by linking the history of their church to the great linear narrative of time. They were aided in the purpose of their task by another element in historiography which had preceded them: the idea of *rhetoric*. The Roman writers Sallust and Cicero had argued that there were rules and codes to follow in writing of all kinds, and specific ones for writing history. The 'rhetor' (or narrator)

5. The Bayeux Tapestry represents the Norman Conquest of England – and can therefore remind us that writing is not the only method for recording history.

of history should tell the truth impartially, even if that offended other people; should arrange things chronologically and geographically; should tell what 'great deeds' were done, paying attention to their causes, including character and chance; and should 'write serenely in an easy flowing style'. The point of the rules was that the history thus written should be persuasive, and well received. This rhetorical element – produced by the Romans, developed by the Christians – had a long historiographical legacy.

In 1067 an anonymous author finished writing *The Life of Edward the Confessor*. He dedicated his work to his patron Queen Edith, wife of the English monarch. His purpose in writing was to praise the Queen's family, and thus Edith herself. He was, however, hampered in his task by the fact that Edward's reign ended in disaster, with Edith's brothers Harold and Tostig quarrelling tragically. His solution was twofold: first, book two of the *Life* deals with Edward's religious life, and suggests that Edward led the path towards salvation in the next world (which more than made up for any problems in this one). Secondly, by effectively blaming familial strife for all the troubles that befell the kingdom, the author uses a form of inverted praise – how important that family must have been, that its own problems led to so many other disasters! What the *Life* does not mention, however, is the Norman Conquest of England in 1066.

The great medievalist Richard Southern remarked, 'a historian who could write about the disasters of 1066 without mentioning the Norman Conquest is evidently not a historian in any very pedestrian sense of the word'. Indeed not! And the writer of the *Life* (as Southern points out) would have felt no criticism from this statement. Although he did not mention the Conquest, because he did not want to belittle in any way the place of Edward's dynasty, he nonetheless conformed to the rhetorical rules of history. His use of rhetoric to play with the 'facts' was not a trick or sham, but a legitimate part of a historiographical *method*. Modern historians who look back to medieval writers are often concerned with how much they can trust them (the question of sources and trust being something we shall discuss in a later chapter). But the writer of the *Life* would have thought this an impertinent question: within his own lights, he was telling the truth. What could be more trustworthy than following the accepted rhetorical rules of history, so that the history written actually did the job it was supposed to do?

In fact, the *Life* appears to us rather more trustworthy than many histories written around the end of the first millennium. Some historians were influenced not only by the idea of rhetoric, but by the detailed models of classical texts. Richer (died c.998), a monk at Rheims, wrote a history of Gaul. His material source was an earlier historian called Flodoard, whose works were at hand in Richer's monastery. His method was to rewrite Flodoard in a more 'classical' style, aiming at the easy rhetorical flow recommended by Cicero and Sallust. The facts – as Flodoard had presented them – were left to fend for themselves as best they could. When a 'pleasing' classical allusion presented itself, Richer allowed it to trample over the rather boring account of reality. The early Capetian kings were presented as Roman Caesars, imperial lawmakers dressed in togas (the reality would have been sweatier, and less well dressed). Richer would not, however, have recognized any problem in allowing style to overwhelm content. That was the point: he (like many other historians) was telling stories to entertain.

As the Middle Ages continued, rhetoric stayed present in historiography, but other elements began to emerge. The accepted tools of the medieval historian's trade were the classical models of composition and rhetoric, and the materials on past events provided by verbal accounts, annals, and other chronicles. Writing history was often simply a matter of stitching together those accepted elements of the past that served one's purpose. However, things began to change. William of Malmesbury (1095–1143), librarian of the abbey of Malmesbury, wrote a number of works of history. The apparent modernity of his working methods might speak to us. He searched out sources and documents (citing them carefully as an historian should) and talked to people to investigate recent events. And he was critical and suspicious – the two modern 'virtues' of historians. 'That I may not seem to balk the expectation of my readers by vain imaginations', William writes, 'leaving all doubtful matter, I shall proceed to the relation of substantial truths'.

William's aim was objectivity and an unbiased account. Two things thwarted this: although critical of his sources, he still had to follow them and thus often unwittingly incorporates their biases. And William wanted to do more than relate what happened; he wanted to explain it too. This involved guessing (the art of good guessing being the third virtue of the modern historian) which in turn necessitated a theory of human nature. William believed that human beings usually acted out of self-interest. He does not condemn them for doing so, but he frequently relies upon this as a causative explanation of events. Again, this is familiar to the modern historian (we trust no one!). But this use of suspicion does not equal objectivity, and William's account of human nature is rather different from our own. Although he judged human nature harshly, he frequently depicts his subjects brought low by fate despite their schemes, and redeeming themselves on their deathbeds, as good Christians should. Part of the account of his histories – what he thought they *meant* – is that God is the ultimate influence on, and cause of, human events.

The twelfth and thirteenth centuries saw then a move away from the strictures of classical models of historiography. A burgeoning group of literate men, both secular and religious, began to produce histories. The topics of historiography gradually broadened to include 'national' and 'World' histories (such as the entertaining and prejudiced works of Matthew Paris), and chivalric histories (such as the fifteenth-century Jean Froissart's *Chronicles*). History was still written for a particular purpose (to flatter a patron, to honour a city, to praise a monarch) but the purposes were becoming broader and more varied. The styles and methods varied too: Froissart wrote to entertain and flatter his aristocratic audience, and thus looks quite fictional. Galbert of Bruges, writing about the murder of the count of Flanders, was trying to understand the import of what had happened for his country; consequently his writing is extremely careful and exact.

Let us look now to the fourteenth century:

> I, Giovanni [Villani], citizen of Florence . . . hold it meet to recount and make memorial of the root and origins of so famous a city, and of its adverse and happy changes and of past happenings . . . to give example to those who shall come after, of changes, and things come to pass, and their reasons and causes; to the end that they may exercise themselves in practising virtue, and shunning vices, and enduring adversities with a strong soul, to the good and stability of our republic.

Italy – Florence in particular – was beginning to fall in love once more with ancient Greece and Rome. The classical tradition had never really gone away, but from the late fourteenth century onwards Italy persuaded itself that it had rediscovered and renewed the glory of ancient wisdom in a way that early centuries never managed. This affected historiography in a number of ways. First, as Villani's introduction to his chronicle of Florence shows, the idea of learning philosophical lessons from the past was once more in favour. Reading later Italian chronicles, we also find that other elements of classical thought had returned: fate governs events, and has a tendency to bring low the rich and famous; history is a storehouse of examples for the politician and ruler; Ciceronian rhetoric is the essential style for the historian. There was a rapid growth in the production of histories, as each city wanted its own account of its link to the ancient past.

We are talking here, of course, about the Renaissance. This was not the term used by those writers for their own time; but they were convinced that their 'modern time' was essentially different from what had gone before, because of its link to antiquity. Historians set out to show that Florence was the direct descendant of Ancient Rome, and that Italian citizens were the true inheritors of classical thought. This new motive for writing history brought with it – almost by accident – a seismic shift in the idea of the past. No longer did historians look upon their present time as the penultimate stage in the Seven Ages of Man. Now they (and we) talked about three periods: Ancient, Medieval, and Modern. Medieval – the 'Dark Ages' – was the poor relation. Although medieval histories were copied and then published in the fifteenth and sixteenth centuries, for the information they rendered about the ancient past, the general feeling was that nothing very much of import had happened between the fourth and fourteenth centuries.

The renewal of ancient learning affected many more areas than history. In fact, historiography was perhaps becoming once more a subset of philosophy and poetry. As we pass through the sixteenth century, rhetoric gains position as the dominant muse. Style once more conquered content. History should not only be written beautifully, but should also deal with only those things and people suited to its 'dignity'. Historians were not interested in 'everyday life' any more than great artists would contemplate painting peasant women.

Rhetoric also invited particular set pieces (rather like the semi-formalized *incandenza* in Baroque music). Ruthlessly following classical models, historians portrayed the 'character' of great men, imaginative and hyperbolic battle scenes, and most importantly, great speeches. Particularly upon entering battle, historical figures in the Renaissance find themselves discoursing at great length and with rhetorical vigour in a manner similar to Shakespeare's heroes. A historian has one commander begin:

> My loyal soldiers and good friends, now is the time for you to wipe out all stain of infamy, if you incurred any in that calamitous defeat of

6. This depiction of Bartolomeo Colleoni, an Italian mercenary captain, displays the Renaissance love of the heroic pose. (Andrea del Verrocchio, 1496)

Varna. Now is the time for you to recover your reputation for loyalty and valour, and to avenge yourselves for so many wrongs and injuries received at the hands of these cursed Turks and unbelieving Mohammedans.

And he continues thus for some time, invoking tyranny, freedom, wives, children, homeland, God, and so on. Presumably the Turks were either waiting patiently for this lengthy speech to finish before starting the battle, or were enjoying a set-piece speech of their own.

After the divisions within Christianity caused by the sixteenth-century Reformation, rhetoric became allied once more to religious polemic. Protestant historians used history to claim first that their religion had much older precedents than Luther (including, as it happened, medieval heretics), and secondly that the Roman Catholic Church had been corrupt for a very long time. Catholic historians pushed back in the other direction. In certain areas, this historiographical fight has never really gone away. But 'history' was clearly being used in the service of its practitioners.

Again, for such historians, this was the whole point. But criticisms did start to emerge during their own time. If history was becoming fictional, or biased, was there any point to it hanging on to tedious things like the 'facts'? And if the point was philosophical – a 'higher' truth than what actually happened – was not poetry already doing that kind of thing rather better? These suspicions began to be directed against the ancient historians and all kinds of history, as well as against early modern polemicists. Sir Philip Sidney (1554–1586) wrote sarcastically of, 'The Historian . . . loden with old Mouse-eaten records, authorising himself . . . upon the histories, whose greatest authorities are built upon the notable foundation of Heare-say'. History was in something of a crisis.

The response came in the form of a series of defences of history. Let us

IEAN
BODIN

7. Jean Bodin, author of the *Method for the Easy Comprehension of History*

pick one: Jean Bodin's *Method for the Easy Comprehension of History* (1566).

> Although history has many eulogists . . . yet among them no one has commended her more truthfully and appropriately than the man who called her the 'master of life'.

These were fighting words! Over a lengthy, detailed, and ruthlessly methodological book, Bodin argued that history was essential for educating society about the correct conduct of warfare, affairs of the state, and government. The idea was not new – remember Herodotus – but the theoretical application was terrifyingly thorough. The *Method* includes a discussion of the relationships between divine, natural, and human history; a method for deciding what to read, based upon the principle that one should move from the universal to the particular; a comprehensive list of historians, arranged by topic, ranging from the Old Testament to recent writers (although including suspiciously few medieval works); and most importantly a chapter setting out how the *reader* of history should be suspicious of past historians, their purposes, methods, and biases.

Bodin, having the virtue of a suspicious mind, appears very 'modern'. But there are differences too: large parts of the *Method* are concerned with discerning essential geographical characteristics of different peoples, based upon history, astrology, humoral theory, and numerology. The 'Truth' Bodin's method aimed at was essentially that of understanding God's divine plan, read through the lens of late-Renaissance 'scientific' learning; much of which now strikes us as bizarre. But for all that, Bodin placed 'Truth' back on the agenda.

So by the end of the sixteenth century, history aimed once again at being a 'true story' of the past. It is important to remember that in each age, there have been other ways in which people have approached the past: in paintings, in music, through objects, in poetry, and literature.

8. Double bust of Herodotus and Thucydides, the ancient Greek historians, the former interested in stories and people, the latter in politics and the state.

Part of the story of this chapter is to show where some of the constituent parts of writing history came from. But part also has been to show that 'history' has always meant different things to different people.

This chapter should not be read as a story of 'progress', about people getting better and more clever at writing about the past. To do so would miss the point. All of these historians were attempting the best understanding of the past they thought possible. We might – from *our* current position – see some of these attempts as more accurate than others. But that is to follow *our* idea of what is 'true'. Past people had different ideas about truth, and what the point was in writing a true story about previous times.

Part of this comes from each author's particular *purpose* in writing history. It has been suggested that writing history is a natural and necessary activity: that history is to society what memory is to the individual. History certainly is very powerful; but if we look back at Nabonidus, or Eusebius, or Galbert of Bruges, or Giovanni Villani, we see people writing about the past because of the specific circumstances and needs of their own time. Richard Southern has suggested that the reason there were particular outpourings of historiography around the turn of the eleventh and seventeenth centuries was because those periods were experiencing particular turmoil and unrest. History served a purpose here: it gave people an identity. In this sense, it is like memory. But *whose* memories? And *which* things to remember?

All of the historians in this chapter tended to choose to remember things in one sort of area: great men, the church, government, politics. In part, this pattern was set by the Greeks: not by Herodotus, who was interested in more varied subjects, but by his successor Thucydides (c.460–400 BC), who wrote a *History of the Peloponnesian War*. Thucydides concentrated on recent events only, where he could avoid the more tricky written sources of the past and rely upon eyewitness testimony and his own experience of the war. He implicitly criticized Herodotus, glossing a correction to the earlier historian's account with the words, 'most people, in fact, will not take trouble in finding out the truth, but are much more inclined to accept the first story they hear'. He baldly stated that history was about politics and the state, and nothing else. Arnaldo Momigliano (a modern author) remarked that having shut himself up in this tower of political history, Thucydides wanted to confine all of us there too. How we escaped from that tower is dealt with in the next chapter.

Chapter 3

'How it really was': truth, archives, and the love of old things

In 1885, at the age of ninety, Leopold von Ranke sat in his rooms in Berlin, composing his last historical works. He could no longer read, his memory was failing him, and he found it difficult to write. Dictating his words to one of his devoted assistants, he set down a brief account of his life as a historian. He talked of how as a young man he had become interested in history: his university lecturers, his readings in philosophy, and his enjoyment of the historical novels of Sir Walter Scott. On the last topic, he said:

> I read these works with lively interest; but I also took objection to them. Among other things, I was offended by the way in which Charles the Bold and Louis XI were treated, which seemed . . . to be completely contradictory to the historical evidence. I studied . . . the contemporary reports . . . and became convinced that a Charles the Bold or a Louis XI as they were pictured by Scott had never existed. . . . The comparison convinced me that the historical sources themselves were more beautiful and in any case more interesting than romantic fiction. I turned away completely from fiction and resolved to avoid any invention and imagination in my work and to keep strictly to the facts.

Ranke is frequently presented as the father of modern historiography. At the heart of this imagined patrimony is his appeal to 'the evidence', his demand that historians could and should produce a 'scientific' and

9. Leopold von Ranke as aged scholar and patriarch

'objective' history if they returned diligently to the documentary archives. His philosophy of history is encapsulated in a much-quoted phrase: 'only to say, how it really was'.

In this chapter, we will use Ranke as our destination, as well as our starting point. There are good reasons (as we will see) for questioning Ranke's claim to fatherhood. There are good reasons (as I will argue) for perhaps wanting to escape from some of the parental influence he still enjoys. But Ranke – an old man, remembering and re-imagining his glorious life as a ruthless adherence to evidential truth – forms a useful terminus. His belief in an 'objective' history makes him seem undeniably 'modern' in contrast to the writers we met in the last chapter. For the purposes of this short account, we will use Ranke as the beginning of modern historiography, and rely on later thematic chapters to elucidate historical thought *after* Ranke.

This chapter, then, will narrate some developments in historiography between the sixteenth and twentieth centuries. It is a complex story. We will meet a number of scholars who would probably not have identified themselves as 'historians', but who nevertheless contributed particular elements to what we now call 'history'. So, to simplify our task, let us take some particular themes as cairns to guide our route: the question of truth; the question of how to use historical documents; and the question of the 'difference' of the past to the present. We can explore each of these themes in greater depth in later chapters. For now, they will mark our path.

At the end of the last chapter, 'history' was under siege in the sixteenth century by sceptics ('Pyrrhonists') who saw it as inaccurate and useless. The 'history' they decried was for the most part a *rhetorical* history, guided by the classical principles of literary composition, and driven by the twin desires to provide a finely wrought narrative, and to present exemplary 'lessons' from past political events. Jean Bodin's defence of history was a philosophical and theological one. But there were other champions of history, who took a rather different route, and whose methods and aims in many ways presaged Ranke's desire for documentary accuracy.

What initially drove forward the defence of 'truth' in history was (as in the early Christian era) religious conflict. It might seem curious that the most all-embracing bias – faith – has been responsible for developing tools designed to produce objective truths. But, when looking at the sixteenth and seventeenth centuries, we are observing cultures that saw factual 'truth' and religious 'Truth' bound together in an inescapable continuum. At stake was not only the truth about the past, but the truth of God.

Both Protestants and Catholics turned to history to support their opposing claims to authority. On the Protestant side, history was used as a particularly partisan weapon, either to claim a longer existence for their creed, or else to vilify the Roman church. Catholicism, which had a more secure past, approached history in a more constructive fashion, attempting to bolster the faith further by returning to its own past for proof of its legitimacy. On both sides, writers turned to documents as a source of proof. For example, the Protestant scholar Flacius Illyricus gathered a team of workers in the mid-sixteenth century. They copied and collated medieval documents as evidence for a long history of Roman Catholic 'corruption', and to claim the existence of 'protestants' before Luther (including, as it happened, the medieval heretics we met in Chapter 1). On the Catholic side, in the mid-seventeenth century, groups of church scholars known as the Bollandists and Maurists compiled ecclesiastical histories and martyrologies, such as the monumental *Acta Sanctorum* ('Lives of the Saints'). These scholars, and others like them, made use of documentary evidence on a grand scale. Their methods were, however, relatively unsophisticated: the point was to assemble a mountain of evidence that would serve as a bulwark against their enemies.

Rather more sophisticated was the analysis of documents carried out by antiquarians. The term 'antiquarian' tends to carry negative connotations nowadays, of someone with a naive or unsophisticated obsession with the past. This adverse view was sometimes also held in earlier times. In 1628, one John Earle (tongue perhaps in cheek) characterized the antiquary as 'one that hath that unnaturall disease to bee enamour'd of old age, and wrinckles, and loves all things (as Dutchmen doe cheese) the better for being mouldy and worme-eatern.' Antiquarians loved the past. There is an important distinction here between 'antiquarian' and 'historian'. We should not imagine these terms to describe discrete groups of scholars; in fact, these people wrote to each other and saw themselves as engaged in common practices. Nonetheless, to generalize broadly, 'historians' wrote

10. '. . . . mouldy and worme-eatern' – Ole Worm's antiquarian cabinet of curiosities (1655)

expansive and entertaining histories, inspired by the Ciceronian model of a grand and educational tale. Antiquarians, in contrast, collected together everything they could lay their hands on connected with whichever period in the past had taken their fancy. They had less a grand tale to tell, than a great love to express.

But it was antiquarians, specializing in a number of different areas, who developed the tools for dealing with the past via its documentary and material remains. Here our second theme comes into play: the use of documents. The initial inspiration for change was once again religion. In 1439, Lorenzo Valla (1406–1457) produced what was perhaps the most famous piece of documentary analysis on perhaps the most famous document in the fifteen-hundred years after Christ. The document was the 'Donation of Constantine', which purported to record the gifts and rights bestowed upon the Christian church in the fourth century by the Roman emperor of that name. The 'Donation' had been the most potent weapon in the Church's armoury throughout the Middle Ages. Valla proved it was a forgery.

Now others had raised doubts about the 'Donation' since at least the twelfth century. But Valla (motivated, it should be noted, by a sincere desire to *hurt* the Papacy) framed his critique in a new way. He concentrated on the *language* of the document. Analysing the style of Latin it employed, and the details it provided, he concluded, with declamatory flourishes, that it was a medieval fake:

> Let us talk to this sycophant [i.e. the forger] about barbarisms of speech; for by the stupidity of his language his monstrous impudence is made clear, and his lie!

Valla was a 'philologist', a scholar of language, and he had noted that the Latin of the 'Donation' was not at all like the 'classical' Latin of the fourth century, from whence it purported to date. Valla describes the Latin of the document as 'barbarous' because, like most Renaissance scholars, he saw everything between late antiquity and his own time as a decline in learning and elegance. Valla was driven therefore by two prejudices: religion and linguistic purity. But this application of philology to historical documents provided two new thoughts on how to address the past. First, one might criticize a document from its internal characteristics, and thus develop some criteria as to what constituted 'truth' in the historical record. Secondly, language (and, therefore, culture) *altered* from historical period to historical period; that what had changed over the course of time was not just the fortunes of the ruling elite, but the ways in which people talked and lived.

This had implications beyond an attack on the Roman church, and relates to our third theme, of how the past differs from the present. Valla saw language as supremely important in shaping society. He understood the Roman 'Empire' to be everywhere and anywhere that Latin was spoken, because the fundamental elements of what made the Romans special were intertwined with the language that they spoke, and the way in which they understood the world. Valla therefore not only placed a milestone on the path to serious documentary analysis; he also reintroduced the study of language and culture into history. The idea that history included more than political 'events' was the first escape from Thucydides' tower of political history.

These ideas and their implications were not full-born with Valla, and did not lead to any immediate revolution in the practice of history. Valla was not a 'historian', and neither were those who developed these themes. They were, instead, philologists studying changes in Latin, scholars attempting to refine Roman law, numismatists who used ancient coins to reconstruct new pictures of antiquity, and chorographers who tried to gather together every detail relating to the past history of a particular geographical area. John Dee (1527–1608) defined chorography as the practice of describing a 'territory or parcell of ground' wherein 'it leaveth out . . . no notable, or odde thing, above the ground visible. Yea and sometimes, of thinges under ground,

11. The antiquarian William Camden

geveth some peculier marke or warning, as of Mettall mines, Cole pittes, Stone quarries etc'. Not perhaps the clearest exposition, but then, in addition to practising chorography, Dee was both a magus of black magic and believed to be involved in Queen Elizabeth I's secret service. We should not be surprised if he tended towards the arcane.

These antiquarian pursuits became increasingly popular across Europe in the late sixteenth and seventeenth centuries as philologists, numismatists, and chorographers grouped together to share their enthusiasms for the 'mouldy and worme-eatern'. Even in the nineteenth century, amateur scholars looked back to these antiquarians and claimed them as their forefathers. Many of the edited documents that historians now use are the product of these Victorian groups: for example, the *Camden Society*, the *Cambridge Antiquarian Society*, and the *Dugdale Society*. The *Camden Society* is named after the most famous English antiquarian, William Camden (1551–1623). His massive work the *Britannia*, written at the end of the sixteenth century, aimed to reconstruct every known detail about Roman Britain from surviving evidence. Camden's aims, and those of his imitators, were not influenced by the Ciceronian model of rhetorical history. He was trying to piece together a picture, not tell a story. But Camden's dedication to historical *evidence*, both written and physical, was later to be incorporated into historiography so thoroughly that modern historians tend to forget to whom they owe this debt.

Antiquarians gave us the tools to investigate documentary evidence. The 'Pyrrhonist' challenge to history had pointed to inaccuracies in historical accounts, and had argued that one should therefore abandon all faith in such documents. The antiquarian response – particularly as it was slowly adopted by historians themselves – provided methods for criticizing the accuracy of past accounts; but it also suggested that careful analysis could allow the scholar of past times to winnow out the truth from the nonsense. François Baudouin (1590–1650) was one scholar attempting to understand how Roman law (and hence systems

12. Map of Britain, from Camden's *Britannia* (1607 edition)

of government) had changed from the past to his present. He saw the possibility of joining historical studies with jurisprudence, to try to 'purge history of fable'. A historian, Baudouin suggested, should be like a *lawyer*: balancing conflicting accounts, trying to establish the exact sequence of events, treating 'witnesses' (documents) with dispassionate and objective suspicion. This may sound strangely familiar; at school, I was certainly taught (perhaps because it sounded exciting) that a historian is like a detective investigating a crime. Lawyers were the 'detectives' of Baudouin's age.

We should not be completely persuaded by this assertion of 'objectivity'. Some historians were impelled by the wars of religion, such as Jacques-Auguste de Thou (1553–1617), whose writings in the early seventeenth century were an attempt (albeit unsuccessful) to provide an 'honest' account of the history of Europe which would soothe religious conflict and lead to stability in France. Others, such as Jean du Tillet (died 1570), were driven to archival research out of a nationalistic desire to establish, historically and philologically, the German ancestry of the French (Germany then being admired as the most ancient nation). So these men had motives; but they did produce new methods and tools, which we have inherited. They worked in the archives with original sources. They saw a distinction between later accounts of events, and 'eyewitness' evidence. They recognized that all historical ages were not the same, that the different ways in which people had expressed their understanding of the world around them could be approached through analysing the language they had used; and they attempted to correct mistakes and to get it 'right'. De Thou, for example, wrote to scholars across Europe showing them drafts of his work, in the hope that they might point out inaccuracies, fill in missing details, and provide proof of the truth or falsity of certain matters. History up to the Renaissance had been something that one composed. History after the Renaissance, informed by methods for work and investigation, was increasingly something that one *did*.

The changes sketched out here might suggest that whereas the historians mentioned in Chapter 2 were creating 'true *stories*', the historians in this chapter aimed at '*true* stories'. It was the period from Valla to Baudouin that developed methods and principles for the use of sources, and tried to establish that the 'truth' of history could be proved through evidence. One effect of these changes was to develop a more nuanced understanding of how the past might differ from the present. However, we must note that the emphasis on 'truth' was not universally sustained after the antiquarian enterprises of the sixteenth and seventeenth centuries. But perhaps we would better understand the complex and interweaving strands of our current tale if we thought of historians constantly wavering back and forth between those two poles of 'truth' and 'storytelling'.

As we enter the eighteenth century, the century commonly associated with what is often called 'the Enlightenment', the 'true stories' of history were being linked to questions of philosophy. This new purpose for history affected the historian's view of past times and historical documents. Voltaire (1694–1778) commented:

> Woe to details! Posterity neglects them all; they are a kind of vermin that undermines large works.

Voltaire's apparent rejection of historical detail might lead us to suspect that Enlightenment scholars had returned to a Pyrrhonist rejection of history. Such a view of the Enlightenment did indeed gain currency in the nineteenth century, when historians of that time were trying to define themselves against their predecessors. But in fact what we have in the eighteenth century is a rather different impetus, the desire to make history *relevant* to the themes that concerned Enlightenment thinkers: Reason, Nature, and Man. Writers such as Voltaire, Hume, Vico, and Condorcet were using a study of the past to address 'big' questions about the nature of human existence and the workings of the world around them. Their interests allowed a second escape from

13. Voltaire, historian, man of letters, philosopher, playwright, and quintessential Enlightenment scholar

Thucydides' tower. Just as in the natural sciences new phenomena were coming under the view of the scientist, so too for the philosophic historian it was insufficient simply to deal with an accumulation of facts and political events. The world – both present and past – was above all else *complex*. Enlightenment historians were interested not simply in the decisions made by ruling elites, but by geography, the climate, economics, the composition of society, the characteristics of different peoples. If scientists could point to the fabulous interconnections of the natural world, historians should try to understand the past in a similarly intricate fashion.

It is very difficult to talk about 'one' view of history during the Enlightenment: as in every other intellectual area, the eighteenth century was characterized not so much by a single mode of thought as by its heterogeneity and love of arguments. (Lionel Gossman has helpfully suggested that when talking about 'the Enlightenment', we imagine it to be a 'language' or common mode of speech, rather than any set of generally assumed principles.) Nonetheless, we can perhaps pick out some main themes as they relate to changes in historiography and the understanding of the past.

First, the past itself: there was a lot more of it. Developments in botany and geology had led various thinkers to the conclusion that the world was much older than the Old Testament would admit. If the biblical account of the Six Days of creation were 'true', it could not be literal but symbolic. This expansion of time itself – although highly contentious – inevitably challenged past assumptions. The role of God in history had to be redetermined. For some writers, He was simply to be dispensed with. For others, His role was imagined as that of 'Divine Providence': the ineffable and perfecting plan that subtly directed the course of human history, and acted as its final cause. 'Providence' did not appeal to all historians, and could lead to some curious assumptions. German historians in the mid-eighteenth century pointed out that a belief in 'Providence' tended to lead some writers (such as the not very talented, but very widely read Johann Hübner) to accepting *any* historical tale that would seem to indicate God's presence. Hübner, for example, included in his history of Mainz the story of the 'Mouse Tower'. In this tale, Hatto, the archbishop of Mainz, had a number of beggars burned alive, and exclaimed 'Listen! Listen to my mice squeal!'. He was subsequently harassed by hordes of aggressive mice, and despite taking refuge in a tower in the middle of the Rhine, was eventually eaten by his pursuers. Hübner argued for the factual veracity of this account on the grounds that there was indeed a 'Mouse Tower' in the middle of the Rhine, the story was very old and well known, it was as valid as any biblical story about plagues of frogs or locusts, and a similar event had occurred (he claimed) in Poland in 823!

Fortunately, not all historians found this methodology of truth entirely acceptable.

But if 'Providence' was to be abandoned, historians still needed a theory of causation. Two competing models presented themselves: chance and Great Men. The former theory played philosophical games with the idea that no great event is planned or intended. Voltaire, in his *Dialogue between a Brahmin and a Jesuit*, traces the cause of Henry IV's assassination to the Brahmin having set off on a walk with his right foot instead of his left. For those who followed the 'Great Men' theory, events occurred because remarkable individuals made them happen. An extreme example from the second camp (and frighteningly devoid of Voltaire's impish humour) is Johann Fichte's (1762–1814) comment on Alexander the Great:

> Tell me not of the thousands who fell around his path; speak not of his own early ensuing death – after the realisation of his Idea, what was there greater for him to do than to die?

The twin beliefs in the overpowering force of 'Reason' as an abstract, transhistorical phenomenon, and the role of the individual genius,

14. Edward Gibbon (attributed to Lady Diana Beauclerk)

burning with the purity of his own philosophical mission, strike frightening chords to modern ears.

The Enlightenment also propounded a belief in the transhistorical universality of human nature. David Hume (1711–1776) wrote that 'Mankind are so much the same, in all times and places, that history informs of nothing new or strange in this particular. Its chief use is only to discover the constant and universal principles of human nature'. Medieval historians had tended to assume that the past was just like the present, but what Hume was expressing was slightly different: not the 'assumption' of transhistorical similarities, but (as he saw it) their *discovery*. History was influenced here by the logic of the natural sciences, which believed that the world was essentially static, and governed by laws that could be understood through careful inquiry. Hume believed that the study of history could similarly uncover those essential elements that made up 'human nature'.

The theme of inquiry brings us back to the antiquarian legacy. In many ways, seventeenth-century antiquarianism, with its emphasis on documentary detail and the historical differences between periods, was in tension with the grander, philosophical history of the early Enlightenment. But the eighteenth century also saw a joining of these two elements, fusing them into something rather more like the history we know today. A great example is the work of Edward Gibbon (1737–1794). *The Decline and Fall of the Roman Empire*, one and a half million words in length, covering European history from ancient Rome to the late Middle Ages, is unlike any other history book we have mentioned thus far. Its topic was not new, although Gibbon's attempt to analyse the course of the decline of a civilization had not perhaps been previously attempted. Its methodology was not new, for here Gibbon was clearly indebted to the techniques of antiquaries. What makes it different is this: it is still read today.

Now, this is a slightly disingenuous statement. Some older historians are also read, the ancient Greeks in particular. And Gibbon is read, but no longer much trusted. But what the *Decline and Fall* presents (and why book clubs still publish lavish editions of it) is a history that fuses together, to pleasing effect, the source-analysis of antiquarianism with the style of Ciceronian narrative, and the inquiry of Enlightenment philosophy. This is not to claim that Gibbon excelled in any of these areas: he never visited the archives, but relied on printed editions of documents; his writing is elegant but sometimes arch; and the big problem with the *Decline and Fall* is that Gibbon never properly tells us why Rome decayed, or what the 'fall' of a civilization might really mean. Nonetheless Gibbon was, if not the first, perhaps the most integrated example of a working *historian*. Not a philosopher, not an annalist, not a chorographer or antiquarian, but a historian.

I have said that Gibbon does not 'explain' the fall of Rome. It might be fairer to say that his explanation is based not in abstract analysis, but in accumulative narration. Rather than subscribing to one mode of causation, such as chance, Gibbon attempts to demonstrate the complexity of historical causation, the myriad interactions between disparate elements. In the *Decline and Fall* this belief in complexity is not a stated theory, but an implicit logic; however, historians in the late eighteenth and early nineteenth century – particularly in Germany – began to develop such theories. They were dissatisfied with explanations of 'chance', as simply giving up in the face of complexity; and they mistrusted the philosophy and politics of those who held to the 'Great Men' viewpoint. As the Scottish writer Thomas Carlyle (1795–1881) later put it:

> Which was the more important personage in man's history, he who first led armies over the Alps ... or the nameless boor who first hammered out for himself an iron spade? ... Laws themselves, political constitutions, are not our Life, but only the house wherein our Life is led; nay, they are but the bare walls of the house: all of whose essential furniture, the inventions and traditions and daily habits that regulate

and support our existence, are the work not of Dracos and Hampdens, but of Phoenician mariners, of Italian masons and Saxon metallurgists, of philosophers, alchymists, prophets and all the long-forgotten trains of artists and artisans.

Historians, particularly from the late stages of the German Enlightenment, were increasingly convinced that to understand history properly, one needed to do two interlinked things: first, to study the archival sources in great detail; and secondly, to develop theories of causation that would draw together the complex relationships between the effects of geographical location, social systems, economic forces, cultural ideas, technological advances, and individual will. History was moving away from politics and law towards economics and what we would now call sociology. One would think from this onslaught that Thucydides' tower was surely in ruins.

We are heading now back to Ranke, whose rejection of the fictionality of history began this chapter. Ranke (1795–1886), as he made abundantly clear throughout his career, saw himself as both innovator and saviour of the historical craft. His call for documentary research and objective historical analysis was presented by many (himself included) as revolutionary and radical, placing history finally and firmly on a 'scientific' footing. As we have seen, however, many parts of this vision were already in place before Ranke's time. Was he therefore no more than a great pretender?

Although a degree – perhaps a large degree – of self-promotion may explain Ranke's image, there is something left to note here about the tendencies of Enlightenment historiography, and what Ranke saw himself as reacting against. Many of the most famous writers of the eighteenth century had produced 'philosophical' histories that were not concerned with the facts themselves, but with how they might illuminate some grand question about human kind and existence. Others had also been inspired by the remaining strands of Ciceronian history, producing beautifully written tales for the reading public (a group that grew considerably in the eighteenth century). All had been informed by what might be the one unifying feature of the Enlightenment: the belief that they lived in a time that was the culmination of Reason, that excelled and surpassed any previous age in knowledge, understanding, and good sense. Enlightenment historians were, at heart, intellectual snobs. They investigated the past with greater or lesser degrees of care, but above all they made judgements upon it. And for the most part, the past did not live up to their high expectations. As one writer put it, 'to regret "the good old days" one must not know what they were like'.

Ranke was suggesting something different. He wanted a careful analysis of the documents, undertaken without imaginative inspiration to 'distort' the findings, subjected to 'scientific' notions of scrutiny and proof, and thus to be able 'only to say, how it really was'. This *image* of the historian as the careful investigator of dusty records, the calm and dry analyst of precise questions, the impartial and stern arbiter of objective truth, remains with us today (although, thankfully, it has been joined by some other, less desiccated, images). Ranke's was not the only path: the French historian Jules Michelet (1798–1874) was also inspired by the archives, but his history was romantic, impassioned, fascinated with the peculiar and marginal, such as witches and heretics. Michelet was not always tremendously accurate; but his flair and imagination provided an alternative inspirational model to later historians.

In any case, Ranke's reality was slightly different from his image. He did use archival sources – though others had been there before him, and in fact about ninety per cent of the references in his books were to documents already studied and published by past scholars. And as with others before him, his aim of objectivity partially succeeded and partially failed. So what did he change? Perhaps two things.

First, if Gibbon, as I have suggested, marks the start of history as a vocation (as something that one chose to do for its own sake), Ranke establishes history as a *profession*. One legacy that Ranke bestowed was the working seminar of historians, where younger students gathered around an established scholar to learn the craft by working directly with primary sources. As far as educational budgets allow, this model still dictates how most young historians learn their trade.

Secondly, the recurrent phrase: 'only to say, how it really was'. This short, innocuous sentence has informed pages of literature on the practice and philosophy of history. It was an attempt by historians (not just Ranke) to escape from the paradigm of the 'true story', to lop off the second fictional term, and to make history simply into what is 'true'. We will discuss this viewpoint further in later chapters. For now, let us note one thing. When Ranke said 'only to say, how it really was', he was in fact quoting a rather more ancient historian: Thucydides. This is where his allegiances lay. Whatever else Ranke gave to history, he returned it once more to the tower of political events. His sources were those of rulers and states, nations, and wars. We have escaped again, but we have been left with divisions, for reactions against the Rankean vision also began a splitting of historiography into disparate components. Few historians describe themselves simply as 'historians' nowadays: we are 'social historians', or 'cultural historians', or 'feminist historians', or 'historians of science', or indeed 'political historians'. This is one reason why the remainder of this book is not going to continue a narrative account of developments in historiography: there are just too many of them, in too many different strands. Instead, we will discover more about twentieth-century historiography in the next chapters through examining certain themes and questions.

It is, of course, ludicrous to suggest that developments in historiography 'ended' in the mid-nineteenth century. My use of Ranke as an end point is in part driven simply by my inability to fashion a coherent narrative from the myriad paths that historiography has taken since that time. But there is some truth to the claim. Since Ranke, historians of every hue have had first and foremost in their minds the idea of 'truth' as something that can be approached or achieved through fidelity to their sources. The claims that history has made for relevance and utility have, since the nineteenth century, tended to rest upon the foundation of careful use of evidence, rather than rhetorical elegance or philosophical acumen.

This process was furthered by the growing institutionalization of history in the nineteenth and twentieth centuries. History was only one amongst a number of subjects that became 'professionalized' after the industrial revolution; indeed, it was rather later in its establishment as a serious topic for university study than some other areas of the humanities. In the late nineteenth century, historians began to form professional groups (such as the American Historical Association) and to start up learned journals. Throughout the twentieth century, growing numbers of historians have studied for doctorates, gained jobs on university faculties, and laid claim to the authoritative status of 'professional'. Part of the drive to professionalization at the end of the last century was the increased economic ability of modern states to support an intellectual class. One effect of this ability was a desire that history should serve the needs of the nation state in producing 'national' histories. These have in part shaped the kinds of historical questions asked by early professional historians in different countries: England saw itself as the pinnacle of parliamentary democracy, and regarded its empire with pride; France looked to the Revolution of 1789 as the creation of the modern state; Germany celebrated the 'superiority' of its culture and race; America gloried in its assumed 'difference' to European models. The professionalization of history did not extricate historians from the needs and partisanship of their particular cultures; if anything, it strengthened it.

Since I have benefited from the professional system, it would seem churlish to bewail it to any great extent. It is, however, worth noting some of the prices historians have paid for professional status. First, there has been an increasing gulf between the general reading public and the academic historian: writing for learned journals or publishing monographs with university presses generally means writing for an audience of under five hundred people. Much that is interesting and important, to *every* reader, is hidden away under an off-putting blanket of professional apparatus. Secondly, becoming 'professionals' has sometimes made historians pretend to an Olympian detachment from, and objective judgement on, the present and the past. We will explore these themes further, but simply note here that 'professional' does not mean 'impartial'; it mainly means 'paid'. Historians now make a living from what they do, which means negotiating the expectations of university committees, funding councils, and peer-reviewed publishers. Historians, like most people, operate within a web of vested interests. Lastly, professionalization has also led to division. Very few historians count themselves as expert on a vast range of areas; they tend to specialize in particular ways. I'm not certain that these divisions are a 'bad thing'; they may be inevitable, and might even be productive. But they do mean that, for us, 'history' (both in terms of what historians do, and the account they render of the past) can never be just *one* true story.

This chapter has explored the development of ideas around the use of sources, the relationship between the past and the present, and the 'truth' of historical accounts. I have sought to show that these questions have a long history, and that the answers to them have varied. If things have been different in the past, so too may they alter in the future: the arguments are not over. We will look further at 'truth' and our relationship to the past later in this book. In the next chapter, however, we will focus in greater depth on sources, and what the historian can do with them.

Chapter 4
Voices and silences

On 1 August 1994, a caretaker working in the Norfolk and Norwich Record Office turned on a light, and the building exploded. A tiny electrical spark in the switch had ignited leaking gas. The workman was blown backwards, but survived. The Record Office did not. Fire-fighters worked to control the blaze, and staff tried to save the documents kept there. When the fire finally went out, 350,000 books and some historical records had been destroyed, and the building gutted.

Why begin here? This chapter, and the two that follow, aim to show how a historian sets about the task of doing history. We are going to trace a true story from history using primary evidence, a story that has not been told before. The job of the historian begins with sources, documents from past times; and the Norwich Record Office (NRO) was, and remains, a repository of these materials (it also happens to be located in the city where I work). Furthermore, when things are placed under threat – such as a fire – they frequently come into clearer view. Fortunately, many more documents were saved than were burned. But the fire did disrupt something almost as important: the classificatory system on which the NRO was run. The surviving records were rehoused, and the Record Office is open once more both to interested amateurs and professional enquirers. But before people could make use of these sources, the NRO had to reconstruct its catalogues, arrange its stock, and recreate its procedures for locating specific documents. The job of the historian begins with sources – but only once the archivist has done his or her job of sorting and ordering those sources for use.

> Historians often refer to historical documents produced at or near the event under investigation as 'primary' evidence (like the 'prime witness' to a crime). 'Secondary' sources indicate the works of other, later writers. However, this is only a useful shorthand, and not very philosophical, because the line between the two can be difficult to draw; and 'secondary' sources are also 'primary' evidence of their own time.

Archives, in the sense of repositories of past documentation, have existed for a very long time. From at least the fifteenth century the citizens of Norwich were concerned to have documents relating to their history stored and kept safe. This was because old documents, particularly those relating to land ownership and legal rights, were forms of power: producing an old (and therefore authoritative) document supporting one's case could help win an argument. This is, of course, still true, as when lawyers search for old documents concerning a house being bought by their clients. But from around the eighteenth century, institutional archives of documents began to be preserved and administered for less clear-cut reasons, kept in part simply because they were interesting. The NRO is just one collection of archives amongst thousands. Most countries have national archive collections, such as the Public Record Office in London, or the Archives Nationales in Paris. Some archives are run-down and almost forgotten, such as one in New York City where, I have been told, homeless people sometimes sleep amongst the stacks. Others are private, belonging to families, companies, or religious orders, and historians have to seek special permission to make use of them. Some are closed and inaccessible, including (until recently) records from the East German Republic and parts of the Vatican's collections. Occasionally parcels of sources are discovered in other places; one historian recently found a wealth of religious documents from the fourteenth century lodged and forgotten in the bell tower of an Italian church. However, such finds are rare; and these things too usually end up corralled into an archive somewhere.

Archives, then, are not simply storehouses. They are systematized repositories of information, cared for and nurtured by professionals. This is important for two reasons. First, the sources of the past do not survive in neat patterns of their own accord. Just imagine if the pages of this book, instead of being bound together in numerical order, were delivered to you as an untidy pile. It would take a long time to make sense of what was being said here! Archivists place the relics of the past into some kind of order, so that others can use them. Secondly, there are huge numbers of surviving sources. The NRO alone houses around two *million* different documents. It would take a historian a very long time to leaf through all of these. Instead, archivists spend time producing what are called 'finding aids'. These are lists of documents, often with brief summaries of what they contain, so that the historian has some idea of what to ask the archivists to bring to him or her.

So what is a 'source'? Until surprisingly recent times, there was something of an exclusive club: sources were assessed by gentlemen scholars for suitable inclusion, passing judgement on their accuracy, 'soundness', and the fairness of their opinions. One source might be said to be 'preferred' – and thus admitted through the sturdy oak doors of historiography – over another. Most of these sources were *narrative* documents: chronicle accounts, memoirs, government records, past histories. Over the course of the nineteenth and twentieth century, this club expanded greatly; sources came to include many more items, such as wills, letters, records of sale and other fiscal accounts, taxation documents, and court records. As we will see later, more sources led to more questions; and more questions to more kinds of sources.

A source can in fact be anything that has left us a trace of the past. It can be a charter, recording a land transfer; a court case, presenting the pleas of the witness; a sermon, given to an unknown audience; a list of books, shares, prices, goods, people, livestock, or beliefs; a painting or photograph of forgotten faces; letters or memoirs or autobiographies or graffiti; the buildings of the rich, displaying their power and wealth, or the buildings of the poor, displaying the opposite; stories, poems, songs, proverbs, dirty jokes, opaque marginal comments made by bored scribes or cunning glossators. A source can be a thousand things; it can be the discoloration of a page in an inquisitor's manual, marked by the imprint of a thousand kisses made in ritual obeisance by those about to be examined. It is a trace of the past.

Let us look at one specific document, from the NRO, and one specific piece of evidence. The document is the Yarmouth Assembly Book from 1625 to 1642. Great Yarmouth is a coastal town in Norfolk, some 20 miles from Norwich. In the seventeenth century the town was governed by a council or 'Assembly' of the freemen, and the Assembly Books record their deliberations and decisions. The document considered here is the sixth surviving book (the earliest dates back to the mid-sixteenth century). It is a large, leather-bound volume, measuring about 30 centimetres by 20 centimetres, containing 536 numbered folios plus some blank leaves. (Folios are different from pages. Whereas we number the face of each page, scribes in the seventeenth century numbered each leaf of paper. Therefore each folio has a 'front' and a 'back', usually now called 'recto' (front) and 'verso' (back). So 536 folios means that many fronts and that many backs – 1072 pages in all.) The pages feel dry and crinkly to touch, and are much thicker than modern paper. The book is so thick (about 15 centimetres deep) one needs to place it upon a specially made pillow to open it, lest the spine gets broken. Although the Assembly Books did not have lists of contents or indexes, the scribes kept the margin free to make brief summatory comments, so that they could locate entries quickly by reading only the margins. The existence of marginal aids indicates that the Assembly

Book was something *used* by the town, as a source of reference, and not simply filled in and forgotten.

The specific piece of evidence is an entry given within the book, on the front (recto) of folio 327, dating from 1635. In the margin it says 'Annuity of 20 marks per annum granted to Mrs Burdett'. The accompanying text reads:

> At this Assembly Mrs Burdett in regard of hir husbands absense from hir, being gone for New England, whereby she is much desitute of means for the maintenance of hir and hir children, petitioned the house for some relief to be afforded hir in supply thereof: which being taken into consideration it is agreed that she shall have 20 marks per annum to be paid quarterlie by the Chamberlines. The first payment to begin at St Michael next: and soe to continue during the good likening and pleasure of the house.

History begins with sources. However, as I have indicated above, historians usually have help in locating specific evidence, if only something to put them onto the trail. In this case, there were two 'beginnings' before reaching this piece of evidence. One was a list of Yarmouth documents in the NRO, which allows one to request the correct volume from the archivist. The other was a generous suggestion from a fellow historian, who told me that the entry concerning Mrs Burdett might be of interest. These are important stages, and something similar is present in *every* history written: a clue that pushes the historian towards a particular set of sources. Historians make choices and decisions before they ever lay eyes on the evidence. So perhaps it would be more truthful to say that *one* way in which history begins is with sources. Another way in which it begins is with historians themselves: their interests, ideas, circumstances, and experiences.

So now we have our piece of evidence. What to do next? Firstly, let us note the skills that historians have to possess. Look at the photograph of

15. Extract from the Yarmouth Assembly Book. Note the marginal comments on the left-hand side, and the folio number at the top right.

the source, and then at the printed version above. The handwriting is not very clear, the spelling archaic, and some of the terms unfamiliar. Evidence must be deciphered. This is to take the first step back towards the past, in trying to understand *what* a long-dead scribe wrote down, even before asking 'why'. The handwriting, with its long looping letters, is a style known as 'secretary hand'. Handwriting has changed over the course of history: in the Middle Ages, handwriting was fairly regular, as most scribes were able to take a length of time over creating documents. But it was also full of abbreviations, familiar to the relatively small group of scribes dealing with documents, but less clear to modern readers. As literacy grew, and documents were created more frequently, handwriting became less tidy and more personalized. By the later seventeenth century, when (in England at least) there was a fairly broad spread of basic literacy, handwriting could be very messy, as people without much formal training hurriedly scribbled down what needed to be recorded. The study of handwriting is called 'paleography', and historians make use of this skill not only to decipher old documents, but also sometimes to date them, as patterns of writing can be roughly linked to particular periods. Other language skills are also useful to historians. Some learn modern languages, in order to read both documents and the works of foreign historians. Some learn archaic languages, such as Medieval Latin, Ancient Greek, Old English or Middle High German, so that they can work on documents in those tongues. Few historians have many of these skills. Instead, through accidents and choices of their personal histories, they tend to specialize.

The handwriting in the Assembly Book is, believe it or not, fairly regular and clear. Some of the 's's look more like 'f's, and some of the 'r's look like 'w's, but otherwise it is probably not much harder to read than the average doctor's prescription. There are a couple of abbreviations, where rather than write all of a word, the scribe has drawn a line above it or written part of it in mid air: for example, in the sixth line 'which' is written 'w^{ch}'; and in the eighth line 'Chamblines' (with a line above) stands in for 'Chamberlines' (or, as we would spell it, chamberlains).

Other oddities of spelling are fairly easy to translate: 'hir' for 'her', 'soe' for 'so', 'likening' for 'liking'. Spelling had not been standardized in England by the seventeenth century, so certain words tend to follow phonetic patterns.

We also need to make a few contextual translations. 'New England' then, as now, indicates the East Coast of America, which was in the process of being colonized during this period. Mrs Burdett was to be paid in 'marks', which is an archaic form of English currency (20 marks was quite a generous amount). 'St Michael next' means 'the next feast of St Michael' or 'Michaelmas', which is the 29th September. We have already noted *what* the document is (a record of civic government). Overall, the meaning of the evidence should now be clear: the Yarmouth Assembly agrees to pay Mrs Burdett 20 marks per year, as her husband has left her and gone to America.

But this in itself is not 'history'. It may be of interest to know that Mrs Burdett was to receive an annuity, but as yet it lacks a context to give it meaning or importance. The murder of Guilhem Déjean, related at the beginning of this book, was perhaps a more exciting story than Mrs Burdett's finances; but that too, we saw, needed to be placed within a larger narrative to have much meaning. What the extract from the Assembly Book has given us is a building block, shaped and ready to use; but the house itself remains to be constructed.

But what kind of house? The historian needs to decide what he or she is trying to build, and what the sources suggest and will support. For which other bricks should we search? We could start looking in a number of directions. We might wish to uncover other annuities granted by the Assembly, and thus create a picture of charitable giving in Yarmouth, in which case we could search through the rest of the Assembly Book (and the other volumes) before perhaps moving on to other civic records from that town. We might, on the other hand, want to trace other instances of people leaving for New England. In this case we would quickly find that although the Assembly Books contains the odd mention here and there, we would be better off with a different kind of source, such as the list of 'persons of quality' leaving for the New World in the seventeenth century, created by order of the English crown. This document lists the passengers of different ships bound for America, their ages and occupations, and includes brief statements about why they had chosen to leave England. Different sources invite different uses, some obvious, some less so. The Assembly Book invites investigation into the civic government of Yarmouth, but it could also be used to discuss society, religion, politics, gender, and so on.

Furthermore, there are other questions to tackle. We need to be certain, for example, that what we are looking at is not a forgery. In the case of Mrs Burdett, this seems unlikely: the extract fits neatly between other entries, written in the same handwriting, and so there is no evidence that it has been interpolated at a later date. Unless we think the whole Assembly Book – a full thousand pages of writing – was forged, there is no reason to distrust the evidence. This is not true, however, of all historical documents; there have been famous forgeries, such as the Donation of Constantine criticized by Lorenzo Valla, and more recently the infamously faked 'Hitler Diaries' that fooled one very eminent modern historian. But unless one is dealing with famous

Forgery: one area of documentation where forgery was common is medieval monastic records. Monks would regularly forge large numbers of charters, setting out the rights and properties of the monastery. This did not always indicate straightforward dishonesty: quite a lot of forgery was done to create documents that 'ought' to have existed, as rights which had previously been accepted by custom later demanded documentary 'proof'.

people or events, forgery is not all that common (because there is little motive for it).

Historians are also taught to think about 'bias' in the sources. Here, however, we need to think quite hard. Part of the reason for the 'gentlemen's club' of sources I described above was an over-concentration on the idea of 'bias'. Looking for 'bias' (the prejudices of the author, and the way they distort the account) may suggest that an 'unbiased' position can be found. This is a problem. If 'bias' is taken to include, as it must, the idiosyncrasies of every human being, there is *no* document which is 'unbiased'. Some sources present their opinions and prejudices very openly, and one must, of course, take account of these, whilst others may need to be studied very carefully for their assumptions. The extract above, for example, seems fairly straightforward – but note that it does not tell us Mrs Burdett's first name. This is probably more than an accident; it is more to do with the assumptions of the scribe and the Assembly, about what details were sufficiently important to record. But note one thing: this 'bias', having been identified, does not need to be 'discarded'; it is, rather, something we can *use*, to tell us about opinions of women and their place, in the seventeenth century. Without 'bias' (were ever such a thing possible), there would be no need for historians. So 'bias' is not something to find and eradicate, but rather something to hunt and embrace.

We also need to think, however, about what the document can and cannot provide. The Assembly Book was written for a purpose, not for our interest and enjoyment: it was there to record the important decisions made by the town. We need to think about what it does *not* say, as well as what it does. For example, although we know that the Assembly decided to grant Mrs Burdett an annuity, we do not know whether this decision was reached lightly or after hours of argument. We don't know whether Mrs Burdett was present or not (she is said to have 'petitioned' the house, but this may mean that she made a request to them before their meeting). We don't know *why* they gave her an annuity, beyond the fact of her husband's absence and her destitution. Historians need to be aware of the nuances of sources, the gaps between what is said and what is not said; their rhythms and syncopation.

It is sometimes said that 'the sources speak for themselves'. This is not true. The extract from the Assembly Book has said little or nothing as yet. But it is perhaps producing a gentle, nagging murmur: who was Burdett? why did he leave for New England? what happened to Mrs Burdett and her children afterwards? To answer these questions we obviously need to track down other references to the Burdetts. Thus we have decided, through a combination of what the source presents, what it leaves silent, and what happens to interest us, on the direction of our enquiry – the particular path we shall follow from our starting point.

There are at least five other mentions of Burdett in the Assembly Book, located by scanning the marginal comments on each page. These add a little to our picture. A 'Mr George Burdett', preacher, appears in 1633 reported to the assembly by one Matthew Brooks, 'for not bowing at the name of Jesus'. A little context is necessary here. There were religious tensions within England at this time, over the nature of the governance and reform of the church. Brooks believed in a brand of moderate Protestantism that supported ceremony, conformity, and royal control of the church. Burdett would appear to be more radical, against royal control and ritual, and therefore did not make ritual obsequience to the Cross ('bowing at the name of Jesus') when in church. Burdett was briefly suspended as preacher on account of Brooks's complaint, but (as a second mention tells us) was then reinstated by the Bishop of Norwich. However, in 1635 Burdett was suspended again for his preaching (which appears to have been both religiously and politically antagonistic) and the Assembly Book records the necessity of finding a new preacher. Two final references tell us that Mr Brooks made a bid to take over the house where Burdett had lived, but that the property was later leased to a Mr Crane for £12 per annum. The last reference in the Assembly Book is to Mrs Burdett's annuity.

So, by putting together further building blocks, we can start to build up a picture of the Burdetts and what had happened to them. For the picture to make sense, one needs some background information – the religious tensions in England, the local politics within Yarmouth – and here we are reliant on the work of other historians. This is no exception to the rule: historians rely on one another's work just as much as on their own investigations into historical sources. If we find something in the evidence on Burdett to challenge the true stories already told about early modern England, all well and good; but it is foolish to ignore what has already been provided as a guide.

To follow Burdett to America – the next part of our story – we need to turn to documents relating to New England. There are, of course, lots of different sources remaining from colonial America. Tracing Burdett through all of them could take a very long time, so what is a historian to do? Well, sometimes that is exactly what a historian does: works painstakingly and tediously through every available document, searching for mention of what interests him or her. Tedious is the key word here. Quite a lot of the doing of history is tedious, and one of the skills of the historian is to continue to operate in the face of that tedium, hoping for the rare moments of discovery. War is sometimes described as long periods of boredom punctuated by short moments of excitement. History is often similar, if rather safer.

But the pleasure of the historian is the moment when something *is* discovered or revealed. Of course, usually historians would search for more than one thing at a time (there is little point in reading all of the colonial documents in search of Burdett if, later on, one decides to search for another person, and has to read them all again). And sometimes, what they are searching for is much more amorphous than a man's name: it might be a particular phrase or way of talking, a

GOV. JOHN WINTHROP
1588 - 1649   SCHOOL OF VAN DYKE

16. John Winthrop, governor of Massachusetts

pattern in the evidence only revealed by later statistical analysis, a process of change that cannot be pinpointed but is made apparent over the length of time.

So how do we find Burdett in the New World? We could look at some of the various genealogical finding aids now available. We could consult an American biographical dictionary, in case Burdett left a lasting mark. We could turn to the indexes of modern books about colonial America, hoping that another historian has already trod part of our path (although only hoping this with the lazy half of our heart, as treading the path for the first time is part of the fun). Or we could look at some of the most obvious and rich sources of evidence for New England, to see, in an idle fashion, whether Burdett happens to pop up . . .

And he does. If one turns to the seventeenth-century *Journal of John Winthrop*, we find a number of references to Burdett. John Winthrop was the governor of Massachusetts in the 1630s and 40s, and both a key historical actor and recorder of history. He originally hailed from Suffolk, coming to America in March 1630 aboard the *Arbella*. His *Journal* is only one part of a large body of evidence relating to New England, known (and published) collectively as *The Winthrop Papers*. The *Journal* has been edited and published in recent years, and includes a voluminous index, which aids our search considerably. Most historians make use of published source material as well as the original archival documents. Although it is often best to see the original document, this desire frequently exceeds the limits of time, patience, and research grant funding. Looking at a published edition has, in any case, its own particular rewards, as it usually means that someone else has done most of the hard, boring work for you, allowing one to pick the tender fruits from the index.

And such fruits they are! From Winthrop's account, Burdett appears in November 1638 ensconced at a place called Piscataqua. He is recorded by Winthrop because once again he was in trouble, having given shelter to some people the governor had expelled from Massachusetts. Colonial America was a politically fraught place, with divisions between those whose allegiance remained firmly with their old countries, and those who were pushing towards greater religious and political self-government. Winthrop, as governor of Massachusetts, was on the latter side; Burdett, it appears, was on the former.

In December 1638, Winthrop recorded the following:

> The governour's letter to Mr Hilton, about Mr Burdett and Capt. Underhill, was by them intercepted and opened; and thereupon they wrote presently into England against us, discovering what they knew of our combination to resist any authority, that should come out of England against us, etc.; for they were extremely moved at the governour's letter, but could take no advantage by it, for he made account, when he wrote it, that Mr Hilton would show it them.

Let us pause for a moment here and think about the vagaries of evidence. First, we need to establish who these other people are. A short bit of digging in the index reveals the fact that Hilton was another Massachusetts politician, and Underhill would go on to lead a rebellion against a Dutch-owned colony. Note that Winthrop, in his own journal, refers to himself in the third person, and so is perhaps aware that he is writing a semi-official account that may be viewed by other people. We are not privy to his innermost thoughts here, but to what he *chose* to record. We must also ask ourselves how Winthrop knew that his letter had been intercepted, and of Burdett's letter to England – and, in this case, find no answer. Finally, there is Winthrop's description of his own letter: written in such a way that its discovery would do him no harm. As far as we know, this letter does not survive, but imagine for a moment that it does: the historian would (without the *Journal* account) have to interpret a letter that presumably said one thing but meant another. Sources are not transparent and innocent documents. They are written in particular circumstances, for particular audiences; in the case of

Winthrop's letter, written in one way for the particular audience of Mr Hilton, and in another surface way for the suspected audience of Burdett and Underhill.

Further entries in Winthrop's journal show a continuing breakdown of relations between Burdett and himself, including in May 1639 the discovery of a letter written by Burdett to William Laud, Archbishop of Canterbury, decrying the colony's attempts at self-government. A copy of this letter survives in other documentation (the State Papers in the Public Record Office in London), and so we can feel more confidence in Winthrop's account by linking it to supporting evidence. By March 1640, Burdett had apparently become the 'governour and preacher' of Piscataqua (a fact related when Burdett prevented a new arrival from England preaching in his area). Finally, in the summer of 1640, Winthrop tells us of the arrival from England of a lawyer called Thomas Gorge, who travelled to Burdett's area. There, Winthrop says, Gorge,

> found all out of order, for Mr Burdett ruled all, and had let loose the reigns of liberty to his lusts, that he grew very notorious for his pride and adultery; and the neighbours now finding Mr Gorge well inclined to reform things, they complained of him [Burdett], and produced such foul matters against him, as he was laid hold on, and bound to appear at their court.

Burdett was fined about £30, whereupon:

> He [Burdett] appealed unto England, but Mr Gorge would not admit his appeal, but seized some of his cattle, etc. Upon this Mr Burdett went into England, but when he came there he found the state so changed, as his hopes were frustrated, and he, after taking part with the cavaliers, was committed to prison.

Again, pause for a moment. Winthrop's account, which gives us this narrative, purports to be a month-by-month annal of his governance of

Massachusetts. But details in this last passage would seem to indicate that he was writing after the event – telling us what happened to Burdett *after* his return to England. These events must surely have happened some time after his court case; and for news of them to have travelled (by sea) back to Massachusetts must have taken some further weeks. Furthermore, 'after taking part with the cavaliers' sounds very much like engagement with the conflicts of the English Civil War, where Cromwell's Roundheads fought the King's Cavaliers. But this fighting did not start until 1642. How then could Burdett's future be known in 1640? Only if the account were written later. Winthrop's *Journal* – like every piece of historical evidence – needs care and attention in its use. Documents rarely set out to trick historians, but they can bamboozle the unwary at every turn.

In any case, we now have another true story from the past, pieced together from documentary sources: of how George Burdett, puritan preacher and possible libertine, fell from grace in Yarmouth, abandoned his wife and children for the New World, rose to some heights in his new home only to be brought low once again, returned to England to take the King's side in the Civil War, and ended up in prison. Where and when does this story end? It finishes when we either run out of sources or run out of steam – but always, in some sense, the latter, since the story of George Burdett might be linked to the story of Captain Underhill, or the story of Thomas Gorge, or the story of religious reform in England, or the story of colonial liberty, or the story of the English Civil War. It is, as it stands, quite a satisfying story. But let us not forget that it still contains holes. We do not know what happened to Mrs Burdett, back in Yarmouth (although we might hope that she and her children had a long and happy life without George, since one can find people with the surname 'Burdett' in lists of the Freemen of Yarmouth from the end of the seventeenth century). We do not know quite how Winthrop gained most of his information, or if he told us everything he knew. Most of all, we do not know everything about George Burdett, who seems to have been intriguingly contradictory: a religious man, who abandoned his family; a church reformer, expelled from Yarmouth for failing to obey the practices of the King's church, but then taking the King's side upon reaching the New World, and returning to fight for the King in the English Civil War; a fiery preacher, but decried by his neighbours for his 'pride and adultery'. We have two items written by his hand: the letter to England, denouncing Massachusetts politics, mentioned above; and another, earlier letter to Archbishop Laud (also in the State Papers). This early letter is dated December 27th 1635, from Salem, New England. In it, Burdett appears to explain *why* he first left for the New World:

My voluntarie exile is exposed to censure; levitie, or dissimulacon or w[hi]ch is worse, is charged upon mee: but the trueth is: my practize was regular, & herein obedience eccli[esiastic]all very reall . . . [T]his I thought to impart, to rectifie yor Grace's judgement of mee & my wayes . . . [His reasons for leaving were]: Impetuous & malicious prosecution, importable expense; the end, tranquillitie in distance: w[hi]ch could I yet injoy in my native countrie, it would exceedingly rejoyce mee.

The general tone of the letter is clear: Burdett wants to clear his name with the Archbishop, presumably so that he can at some point return. The detail is less so, not least because of Burdett's florid and pompous style. The reference to the 'importable [i.e. unsupportable] expense' of 'malicious prosecution' would seem to indicate a court case: and, indeed, searching the Calendar of State Papers (a fairly detailed finding aid) we discover Burdett being prosecuted for religious irregularity in the court of High Commission during 1634 and 1635. We therefore know more about Burdett's reasons for departure, but this does not answer all our questions. We still do not really know why he chose to leave his family, rather than defend himself at home. At a certain point, the sources fall silent, and the historian must begin to make some guesses – that is, to *interpret* the documents.

We have no statement about George Burdett's feelings towards his wife and children, but we are told that his departure left them 'destitute', and that he was accused of 'adultery' in New England. Might we then suppose that all was not well with the Burdett marriage? This could be a good guess – it fits the evidence – but it must be a *guess* nonetheless. What then of Burdett's activities on his return to his homeland? If Burdett's choice to fight on the side of the King presents us with a change of heart, we might point to Burdett's experiences in the colony: a brave new world, seeking to free itself from the control of the old country. Did, perhaps, this partial realization of Burdett's vision appal him in its concrete reality? Or having come to his new home, was our preacher immediately looking for ways of return and hence saw it politic to reposition his allegiances, against the colonists and for his monarch? Both are good guesses, and one might take a little from each. We cannot know for sure; but we can progress along our narrative trail having built these little bridges. But we should be clear that the bridges are of our own construction. Certainly we can cite evidence in their support, but not at the expense of disclaiming a role in their building. The historian has to make these little bridges, but he or she cannot and should not forget who placed them there and why, or ignore the fact that each bridge may demand a small toll: the price of continuing down a satisfying path, which may close off or render unnavigable other possible trails.

For there are other guesses we could make. Burdett may have loved his wife dearly, been much pained by parting from his children, and wished to bring them with him only to be thwarted by either their wishes or the expense of the move. Winthrop's report of Burdett's lechery may be no more than a calumny against a political enemy, just as Burdett claimed in his letter to Laud that what had been said against him in Yarmouth were lies. Historians of the English Civil War tell us that the Parliamentary and Royalist sides did not divide equally on grounds of religion, so perhaps Burdett found no surprise in his chosen allegiance. One can continue in this vein – but eventually a choice must be made, a path followed, a guess rendered sufficiently firm to walk upon. However, each guess should be remembered as such. Walk upon too many suppositions, and we may be lost.

The sources do not 'speak for themselves' and never have done. They speak for others, now dead and forever gone. Sources may have voices – plural – which can suggest directions and prompt questions, leading to further sources. But they lack volition: they come alive when the historian reanimates them. And although sources are *a* beginning, the historian is present before and after, using skills and making choices. Why *this* document and not another? Why *these* charters and not those? Moreover, why look at charters and not trial records? Why study government accounts and not diaries? Which questions to pursue, which paths to take?

This is not to suggest, however, that the direction of the true story is entirely determined by the whim of the historian. Documents suggest certain directions to follow, as our search for Burdett has shown. Sources can also surprise, present bumps in the road that reveal new paths previously unconsidered. Reading Winthrop's journal, one's glance cannot help but pass on to items below those searched for. And thus, immediately after Winthrop's second mention of Burdett, one reads:

> The devil would never cease to disturb our peace, and to raise up instruments one after another. Amongst the rest, there was a woman in Salem . . . who had suffered somewhat in England for refusing to bow at the name of Jesus . . .

Refusing to bow at the name of Jesus – like Burdett – catches one's eye; but also the conjunction of the devil, a woman, and Salem (in the later seventeenth century, Salem was notorious for witchcraft trials, and a number of women were executed there). This little hook having sunk in, one then finds, whilst flicking forward to the next mention of Burdett, another instance of a woman hanged at Boston, having been 'so possessed with Satan, that he persuaded her (by his delusions, which she listened to as revelations from God) to break the neck of her own child, that she might free it from future misery'. Horrifying – but intriguing . . . so one starts to search for other instances. And thus a new story begins, its starting point brought about somewhere between the voices of the sources and the interests of the historian.

The historian does not simply 'report from the archives'. If he or she did, they would most probably repeat half-truths and confusions, if not indeed downright lies. For sources are not innocent; their voices talk to certain ends, intend certain consequences. They are not mirrors of past reality, but events in themselves. John Winthrop, we may guess, did not like George Burdett, and he tells us (through the voice of another) that Burdett was an adulterer. Is this the whole truth? Whether it is or is not, why did Winthrop decide that it should be written down and recorded? To place something in writing – particularly at any point prior to this century – should be seen as an extraordinary event, and therefore in need of explanation. Does Winthrop's antagonism (a political antagonism, perhaps, rather than a personal one) invalidate his evidence? If it does, do we abandon the true story of George Burdett, and consign him to the silence of the past? The historian makes a choice, and continues with the tale.

And always there are new questions to ask. Why? Because of new ways of looking, because of other things seen before or after, because of different paths travelled. But primarily because there are gaps, spaces, elisions, silences. The sources do not speak, and they do not tell all. This is, as a French historian recently put it, at once the impossibility and the possibility of history: that history, which aims at the whole truth, cannot ever reach it (can only ever be a true *story*) because of the myriad things which must remain unknown; but that it is this very problem which allows – or rather, demands – that the past be a subject for *study*, instead of a self-evident truth. If there were no problems with discovering what happened in the past, there would be no need for historians (whether professional or amateur), and thus no history – just 'what happened' without dispute or question. History has a beginning in sources, but also in the gaps within and between sources. When the Norwich Record Office burnt down, it was a potential tragedy. In fact, most of the older documents stored there survived, although the fire did consume newspapers and photographs which cannot be replaced. I suggested at the beginning of this chapter that when things come under threat, they often come into clearer view. So perhaps another thing is now revealed: archives must burn down (symbolically of course) for history to happen. We must have sources – but we must have silences too.

Chapter 5
Journeys of a thousand miles

A proverb has it that 'a journey of a thousand miles begins with just one step'. Reconstructing something of the history of George Burdett has given us that first step. Where shall we now travel?

The journeys that historians take, and the stories that they tell of their wanderings, vary in length. It is perfectly possible to tell the tale of Burdett's life, such as we know it, and have done with that. But every life intersects with others, and these histories with larger changes still. We are tempted by the open spaces of long journeys, by the possibility of finding meanings and exploring arguments in our greater travels. Burdett is part of at least two larger stories: the English Civil War, and the colonization of America. We might like to know how it is that England came to internal conflict, and we might seek to understand the effects – on the people involved, and on later parties – of colonizing a brave new world. We may also think about how Burdett fits into these stories – or, indeed, changes them. To do so, we need to find a way to tell such large tales.

Making histories involves guesswork of several kinds. We have already met the process of trying to 'fill in the blanks' within surviving evidence. What this chapter will explore is a further process: how to synthesize larger amounts of material, and what to make of the contours presented by bigger stories. In doing this, historians are aware of change over time, but also of continuities, and they try to explain these things. They are also aware, however, of those whose feet have trod the path before, of other historians' accounts and arguments. These must be dealt with too: agreed upon, demolished, or ignored. The process of creating a story is not simply that of placing one brick upon another, until a structure arises; it involves deciding the causes and effects of the things described, negotiating what has already been said by other historians, and arguing for what the story *means*.

Let us start with the English Civil War. Historians build up an account of the war through surviving evidence, just as one recreates an account of Burdett from the Assembly Book. But this involves, of course, very much more work – and some more difficult choices. The kind of evidence one focuses upon will undoubtedly affect the story told. If, for example, one looks mainly to narrative accounts, royal documents and parliamentary papers, the story that appears is overtly political: of how the monarch Charles I was involved in a web of political, economic, and religious tensions during the second quarter of the seventeenth century, leading to an outbreak of war in 1642 between crown and parliament. Charles was executed in 1649, and for a short while England was governed by parliament, until Oliver Cromwell assumed the position of 'Lord Protector' (a curiously regal position for a republican leader). In 1660, Charles II regained the English throne. This is a story primarily of events: the execution of a king, the battles fought between the sides, the internal politics of the Commonwealth, the victory of the new monarch. Political historians have to explain, to some degree, what caused these events, and the answers they provide vary somewhat, according to their interests. Nonetheless, most agree that Charles I was a rather incompetent monarch, unable to hold together the support of his lords; that there were tensions between different ideas of 'government', notably between a monarch who had sovereign control of his polity, and a more mediated system where parliament had greater say; and that events abroad (particularly in Catholic Ireland, but also on the continent) affected what happened in England.

In this 'political' story, what are the causes of change, and what does it *mean*? It is unfair and inaccurate to lump all political historians into one camp. However, it might be reasonable to say that within the 'political' story, change comes about through human competence or incompetence (an incompetent Charles I, a competent – in the beginning – Cromwell); it is affected by the strength of ideologies (monarchy vs. republicanism), and is subject to a degree of chance (when battles are surprisingly lost). It may well also form part of a 'Grand Narrative' (that is, a very large story, running over several centuries), such as the development of parliamentary democracy. The 'meaning' claimed for such a grand narrative is – as was mentioned at the end of Chapter 3 – the 'superiority' of English political culture. This kind of meaning may be stated explicitly, or may lurk within the structure and commentary on the story told. For some political historians, the causes and meanings of things do not need explicit statement: simply relating the course of events is enough. Narrative, they feel, makes 'what happened' sufficiently clear in itself.

At its crudest, political history remains stuck in a later nineteenth-century mould: narrating 'great events', and passing judgement on 'Great Men' (or their flipside, 'Really Awful Men'). Whilst it would seem churlish to deny that there were and are some men and women (although curiously the latter are less frequently mentioned) who might be called 'Great', it is less clear on what grounds exactly that epithet should be applied, and whether it tells us anything about the person in question, or rather more about the tastes of the historian doing the labelling. At what point, for example, does 'Greatness' wear off, and simple 'competence' begin to apply? Do 'Competent Men' play no role in history? And whose choice of 'Great Men (and Women)' are we talking about? Some of my favourites are Anna Comnena, a twelfth-century Byzantine princess who wrote the *Alexiad*, one of the most beautiful works of history; Mennochio, a seventeenth-century miller, who challenged the inquisition with his very individual ideas on God and creation; and Emma Goldman, an anarchist active at the beginning of this century, once described as 'the most dangerous woman in America', and whose comment on the Russian Revolution was to say 'if there's no dancing, count me out'. I have cast-iron arguments for why these achieve 'Greatness' – but I'm sure that you have equally valid reasons for your own personal choices. Either there are surprisingly large numbers of 'Great Men' around – or perhaps the game of ascribing greatness is more akin to picking your top ten records of all time.

More importantly, 'Great Men' theories of historical causation – and, indeed, theories that deal with the decisions made by not so great men – depend upon a belief that what causes events is the good or bad decisions taken by the individual in power. It is foolish to deny that political leaders wield power and that the choices they make affect the lives of others; but is it not equally foolish to forget the reactions and choices made by the rest of the people in general? Battles may be won by expert commanders, but they are also won by those willing to fight and die, by ideas that inspire people to combat, by the economic systems that support those troops, and by the manufacturing bases that provide their weapons. How often, in any case, does a single battle alter the course of events? The English Civil War involved many battles, and multiple conflicts – so perhaps the question to ask is how it was that people were willing to continue fighting?

What happened in the past is undoubtedly affected – even dictated – by the decisions that people make. But what people intend to do, and what the outcomes of those intentions actually turn out to be, are not often the same thing. Time scale is a factor here: when, in 1517, Martin Luther nailed his ninety-five theses to a church door in Wittenburg he certainly intended to protest against certain activities within the Catholic church (as indeed, had many people, employing the same method of publicity, before him). It is less certain, however, that Luther intended to change the religious shape of Europe, or put into motion countless wars of religion between Protestant and Catholic. Not that Luther could be held solely responsible for all that followed: because his ninety-five theses had an *audience*, and their choices (and the unforeseen consequences of those choices) also affected matters. Furthermore, those choices, and those consequences, were played out within a context of social structures, economic changes, and cultural ideas.

Thinking about society can return us to the English Civil War. Social historians tend to concentrate upon rather different evidence from political historians: in particular, the bureaucratic, localized records wherein one is more likely to find information relating to the common people. Some of this information may permit economic analysis – if, for example, one looks at tax returns, lists of merchandise and sales, records of income and outgoings. Economic pictures of change have had increasing interest for historians in the twentieth century, largely because of the influence of Karl Marx. A classically Marxist account of the civil war tells of a class conflict between a rising 'middling sort' (yeoman, merchants, the wealthier members below the nobility) against the established elite (the gentry, the lords, the King). In this big story, the war becomes part of the overall 'transition to capitalism' (another 'Grand Narrative'): the major, long-term change from a 'feudal' society, run by tradition and hierarchy, to a capitalist one, where wages replace duties, and the pursuit of individual profit over-rode traditional conservatism. Marxist interpretations of the civil war (and, indeed, of much else) have fallen out of favour in recent years, in part because they have sometimes tended to shoe-horn a complex picture into an overly schematic model, but also because Marxism in general has apparently been discredited by the collapse of the Soviet Union (an argument which conveniently forgets the continued existence of communist China, Cuba, and a host of other countries).

Marx is remembered chiefly, of course, as a political thinker. But he and his partner Friedrich Engels were also interested in the interpretation of history; in trying to explain how and why changes occur in societies over long periods of time. His influence on historiography has probably been greater than anyone else's in this century. Although it took a long time for historians to catch up with Marx's thoughts about society, economics, and culture, he came to be extraordinarily useful to social historians. In England, from the 1930s onwards, Marxist historians began writing energetically. Men and women such as Eric Hobsbawm, Dorothy Thompson and, pre-eminently, E. P. Thompson passed this influence on to American historiography. In France and Italy, Marx had a profound impact across the social sciences, whilst Germany has retained a somewhat schizophrenic relationship with one of its most famous sons. In Russia, Marx's influence (or rather, one version of that influence) on historiography was imposed to the detriment of any other viewpoint.

Practically all historians writing today are marxists (with a small 'm'). This does not mean that they are all 'left-wing' (far from it) or that they necessarily recognize or remember the debt. But one key element of Marx's thought has become so ingrained in historians' ideas that it is now practically taken for granted: the insight that social and economic circumstances affect the ways in which people think about themselves, their lives, the world around them, and thus move to action. This is not to suggest that they are completely *controlled* by these circumstances. Marx himself wrote that:

> Men make their own history, but they do not make it just as they please; they do not make it under circumstances chosen by themselves, but under circumstances directly encountered, given, and transmitted from the past.

Almost any interpretation of the English Civil War, or any other topic, will take for granted the utility of examining the society within which things took place, the economic positions and interests of the people involved. Not every historian will go on to talk about 'class', or changes from feudalism to capitalism; but they are, for example, interested in the 'rise' (usually meaning the rise in economic and political influence) of particular groups, whether the 'gentry', the 'middling sort', or the 'middle classes'. Social historians have produced various interpretations of the Civil War, not necessarily reading it as a 'transition to capitalism', but noting that economic changes during the seventeenth century (particularly a rise in population, inflation in prices, and a change in directing production from local to national markets) caused greater social stratification, impoverishing certain people and enriching others. These changes led to a perception of social instability which undoubtedly affected the political situation.

Although social history usually keeps one eye on economic elements – thinking, for example, about how material conditions might be influencing changes in society – its areas of interest are broader. Apart from studying the movement of goods and incomes, social historians also use further evidence – pre-eminently legal records – to analyse the thoughts, feelings, and behaviour of the general populace. Sometimes, this leads historians into different directions, asking other questions. The influence of anthropology and sociology has allowed social historians to investigate the patterns of behaviour they perceive in people's daily lives: their family structures, their conduct in daily life, the way they arrange and give meaning to the social spaces around them. Looking at these areas can lead historians towards different journeys, different questions: why did marriage patterns change? How did perceptions of gender affect social behaviour? A number of books on English society in the seventeenth century do not mention the civil war at all – for them, it is part of a different story, one which did not particularly affect the changes that interest them. A different kind of 'Grand Narrative' has been forged from these analyses, which claims to identify relatively stable structures to society, continuing over several centuries. This sort of story suggests that the life of a field-worker in the fifteenth century was not really very different from that of a field-worker in the eighteenth century, despite the apparent changes in political constitution and governance.

Historians have also, in recent years, become increasingly interested in culture. This, again, has come from the influence of anthropological ideas. At the end of the nineteenth century, anthropology and sociology were, like history, becoming 'professionalized'. This led to a division between these different approaches to the study of human life and behaviour, as each tried to stake specific claims for 'their' field. In more recent times, however, the disciplines have been drawing closer together once again: various anthropologists have become interested in analysing historical periods, and many historians have engaged with the more theoretical insights of anthropology. 'Culture', as it is understood in this context, does not simply mean music, plays, literature and so on; it is taken to indicate patterns of thought and understanding, modes of language, rituals of life, and ways of thinking. Cultural historians have taken Marx's idea, that economic circumstances affect the way people think and behave, and have changed its emphasis: arguing that the *ways* in which people think affect their relationship to society and economics. Getting at the ways in which people think can involve studying the art and literature of a certain period. But it can also be examined by analysing the language and behaviour found in documentary sources.

The historian David Underdown performed such an analysis for the Civil War, looking at the different ways in which parts of English society saw themselves (some of which varied according to geographical location), and the thoughts and fears they had about the world around them. Religion played an important role here: in particular, the difference between the traditional protestantism supported by the established church, and the more radical 'puritanism' preached (in Underdown's view) by some of the 'middling sort'. The former group, largely drawn from the gentry, emphasized obedience and ritual, and believed in a harmonious, hierarchical, and essentially *static* social order, regulated by 'custom'. The latter, associated with a rising 'middling sort', rejected 'papist' rituals, disliked state control of the church, and saw society as fractured and divided, in need of *reform* by the godly (i.e., themselves). We met these tensions in the previous chapter, between Brooks and Burdett.

However, the religious differences can also be seen as part of a wider culture. Non-religious activities, such as football, became part of the struggle: to the traditionalists, football (which usually involved a very violent game between two parishes) was a way of reinforcing feelings of neighbourhood and local community; to the radicals, football illustrated disorderly violence and the need for the lesser sort to be 'reformed'. The question of whether society was stable or in crisis, harmonious or fractured, infected various areas of thought. Underdown finds conflicts within, and between, local areas over 'rights', 'duties' and 'customs', where people were struggling over *different* visions of how the world worked. The harmonious image of society – and hence the kingdom – was sometimes compared to the household, with the husband firmly in control at its head. Interestingly, people in seventeenth-century England were very worried about the household too: there was a concern that 'proper' gender relations were adrift, as women were feared as 'scolds' and (sometimes) 'witches', placing men under their control. Overall, there was a strong feeling that English society was unstable: that 'the World was turned Upside Down'. The idea of 'order' could not be divided into separate compartments labelled 'political', 'religious', and 'cultural'; they were linked together. And hence (in Underdown's assessment) a large part of the civil war was a struggle between two different cultures, two different ideas about how the world should work.

David Underdown's 'true story' of the English Civil War has been challenged by other historians (mainly on the accuracy of the regional and class variations he ascribes). But his mode of analysis provides us with a good example of how thoughts about economics, politics, social structures, and culture can be used together in one analysis. This should not really surprise us: whether academics are labelled 'historians', 'economists', 'sociologists', or 'anthropologists', all are nonetheless engaged in analysing how people exist and interact. Different approaches may carry different emphases, focusing on what each discipline takes as being most interesting or important, but the

THE
VVorld turn'd upside down:

OR,

A briefe description of the ridiculous Fashions
of these distracted Times.

By T.J. a well-willer to King, Parliament and Kingdom.

London : Printed for *John Smith*. 1647.

17. The World Turn'd Upside Down: inversions of gender, society, and the body were linked to the political troubles of seventeenth-century England (1647)

professions have much more in common than they are sometimes willing to admit. History is also increasingly trying to give something back to its sister subjects, rather than simply borrowing their ideas. One thing history can provide is a prompt to think about why and how things *change* over time. Underdown's account is interesting in this regard, since it does not see society as static or stable, but chooses to emphasize how fractured and divided it was, and seeks to draw out those elements that were particularly *contested* in the seventeenth century.

We will talk more about analysing the 'ways in which people think' in the next chapter; for now, let us return to the bigger question of how historians set about making larger stories. We often find ourselves talking of 'causes', and sometimes also of 'origins'. These are useful, common-sense expressions, for getting at complex processes; but they have dangers attached. Searching for the 'origins' of, say, the English Civil War (as a number of historians have done) is tacitly to claim that before a certain point, the event would not have happened. This may be true, if we see the following events as *one* story; but if we admit to the variety of tales that can be told within seventeenth-century England (religious conflict, political ideals, social and economic change) the idea of an 'origin' becomes more difficult. Could there, in any case, be an *English* civil war before there was an 'England'? In which case, the historian must decide at what point such an entity could be said to exist (which is a *very* knotty problem, leading one back at least into the fifteenth century).

'Origins' are preceded by other stories; and events are followed by further events. Take, much more briefly, the colonization of America by Europeans. We can point to factors that caused this process – again, religious conflict, economic forces, ideological motives – but must be aware that in producing 'one' story of colonization, we are synthesizing thousands of individual narratives (like that of Burdett) which may not fit our overall model. Synthesis always involves silencing something; in the second and third chapters of this book, we have a synthesis of over two thousand years of historiography. One must be aware that, given more space, this story would look much more complex than my brief account. Synthesis is useful and unavoidable – but it is still a 'true *story*' and not the whole truth. In recent years, historians (and, arguably, society in general) have become suspicious of the 'grand narratives' formed by synthesis, since these stories tend to trample over the complexity of any particular situation. We are rather less persuaded than we used to be by the meanings ascribed to these grand narratives. The end of the nineteenth century tended to see history as a narrative of 'progress', with nineteenth-century society at, or close to, its apogee. The end of the twentieth century, after two world wars, the arms race, increasing divisions between rich and poor, diseases resistant to human intervention, chemical pollution of the world around us and so on, has rather less belief in 'progress'. This is not to argue that the opposite is true – that things are in terminal decline, which would be another 'grand narrative' – but to note that, in tackling the problems which face us, we have become suspicious of people spinning us great tales, and wish to pay more attention to the details of true stories.

'Effects' are no less complex than origins. Some of the effects of the colonization of America would be the deaths of hundreds of thousands of native Americans, the development and continuation of slavery, the beginnings of England's economic decline over a very long period of time, the establishment of new ideas about government and politics, the cold war, the space race, the multinational society in which we now live. Who could say that the Pilgrim Fathers imagined such outcomes? And who would dare to draw a line under those effects, and say 'this is where the story ends'? For nothing ever ends, really; stories lead to other stories, journeys across a thousand miles of ocean lead to journeys across a continent, and the meanings and interpretations of these stories are legion. 'Origins' are simply where we choose to pick up the story, dictating (and dictated by) what kind of story it is we wish to tell. 'Outcomes' are where we wearily draw to a close.

In trying to decide what 'causes' something to happen, historians can draw on a number of different theories, and fall back into a variety of positions. Most would admit that, except at the most simple level, everything has a plurality of causes. And what then happens on account of those causes becomes, in turn, the cause of something further still. Historians try to make patterns from these intricate series of events; sometimes very simple patterns, such as a narrative of 'important' men, and sometimes very complex patterns, of ideologies, economics, and cultures. There are undoubtedly patterns to be found in the past, but how much they are patterns already present, and how much they are patterns drawn by the historian, is unclear (something we will discuss further in the final chapter of this book). People in the past had their own patterns of how life worked, sometimes conscious and sometimes not. But these patterns – family, gender, political order – were also localized and particular. In drawing meaning from these patterns, historians are involved in making choices about what *they* think is important.

We have examined the different approaches historians take to the civil war as if they formed neat teams, each dressed in the ceremonial garb of his or her tribe, whether it be political, social, or cultural. This, of course, is to oversimplify the picture: any particular historian may have an interest in various forms of explanation, and may see some utility in applying both social *and* cultural forms of explanation, or looking to both the political and the economic. Indeed, we might feel that in trying to 'explain' the English civil war we might want to pick a little bit from several of these bigger stories. Nonetheless, historians do divide themselves into teams, even if they like to ascribe these divisions to others rather than admit to them personally. And when reading historians' accounts of this, or any other, historical topic, it is important to know that they do tend to adopt one of these 'tribal' positions. There is not, and will never be, one sole explanation for the war. To desire one is perhaps to miss the point of the past – that it is *complex*, and therefore demands our care and attention. Every history is provisional, an attempt to say something in the face of impossible complexity. There is a weight of responsibility here on the historian: never to try to claim that his or her account is the *only* way of telling the story. But there is responsibility for the reader also: not to discount histories, because they are imperfect, but to engage with them as the true stories they can only be.

I suggested at the beginning of this chapter that Burdett's story could be one step on the way to a longer path. But just as every journey of a thousand miles begins with one step, so also does it *end*. Burdett presents a fascinating case study in the context of seventeenth-century England and America. His faith and his circumstances led him overseas, but also back home. As a preacher – and a radical puritan one at that – he undoubtedly added to the cultural melange of conflicts and tensions present in the early modern world. But, despite the direction of his faith, on his return he took the side of the King. If Burdett can stand in for a moment for the other thousands of lives we have not examined here – and the many thousands more for which we lack detailed evidence – we can finish with one thought. Without George Burdett, there would have been no civil war; not because he was a 'Great Man', but precisely because he was *not*. Lacking the contrary decisions of Burdett, the complex stories which he found himself playing out in so individual a fashion, there would have been no conflict. History is, as Marx said, made by people in circumstances beyond their own choosing. But they *affect* those circumstances, in the lives they lead. 'Circumstances', 'history', and 'people' are not different things. They go on and on together, awaiting the historian who chooses to draw one pattern from the rest. The pattern which *I* favour is that of unintended consequences: that most, if not all, of what happens is the result of people trying to achieve certain ends, but never possessing the perspective to see what the effects will be. People do things, for reasons and within circumstances linked to their own present. But the things that they do cause ripples, spreading outwards beyond their own moment, interacting with ripples from a million other lives. Somewhere, in the patterns formed by these colliding waves, history happens.

Chapter 6

The killing of cats; or, is the past a foreign country?

The killing of cats has a *history*. That is to say, it is an activity that has changed over time, and hence can be described and analysed by historians, as can activities such as marriage, religion, eating, navigation, genocide, catching fish, cross-dressing, smelling things, and sex. A very brief history of cat killing would read something like this: in Ancient Egypt, cats were revered and honoured, and so when their masters and mistresses died, the felines were walled up in their tombs to keep them company, and thus asphyxiated. In the early Middle Ages of Europe (c.400–1000), cats were much less respected, and mostly died natural deaths, such as from starvation. In the later Middle Ages (c.1000–1450) the feline passed to the other end of the spectrum, and became associated with the devil. Kissing a cat on the anus was understood to be a common habit amongst Cathars and other heretics – or, at least, that is what their persecutors alleged. Some Cathars also believed in the demonic connection. One man claimed that when the inquisitor Geoffroi d'Ablis died, black cats appeared on his coffin, indicating that the devil had come to reclaim his own. So, in medieval times, cats were killed because they were feared, despatched by, for example, having stones thrown at them. By the seventeenth century, the public image of the cat had further deteriorated: it was understood to be the familiar of witches, and was therefore executed along with its mistress or master. In eighteenth-century France, on occasion, large numbers of cats were massacred in mock rituals by apprentices and

18. Killing cats (and mistreating other animals) in the eighteenth century. (Hogarth, *The Four Stages of Cruelty*)

others, who thought the killing very funny. In our own enlightened twentieth century we do not, of course, kill cats; except by neglect, over-feeding, and when it is for their own good.

In the last chapter we described historians as belonging to various different tribes: political, social, cultural. But we also noted that, although these labels are given and accepted by historians (used, for example, when advertising academic jobs) they are not hard and fast boundaries. There is, however, one core difference that divides all historians into two groups: those who believe that people in the past were essentially the same as us; and those who believe that they were essentially different. You might remember this division from our earlier chapters: David Hume thought that all 'men' were so much the same in every age; L. P. Hartley suggested that the past is a foreign country where they do things differently from us. Given that the death of felines does not normally cause hilarity in our present day, an account of eighteenth-century apprentices finding humour in killing cats can provide us with a good example to think through this dichotomy.

We know about what the historian Robert Darnton has labelled 'the Great Cat Massacre' from an autobiography (semi-fictionalized but generally believed to be authentic) written by a printer's apprentice called Nicolas Contat in Paris in the late 1730s. Whether or not Contat's account is literally true, Darnton argues, it nonetheless shows us a story which Contat expected to be read and *understood* by his contemporaries. Documents can show us a 'truth' beyond 'what actually happened': they can demonstrate *how* people think, the images and language and associations they can drawn upon from their culture.

What Contat described was this: two apprentices, Jerome (Contat's fictional self) and Léveillé, lived and worked in a printing shop owned by their master, Jacques Vincent. The master's wife adored cats, having a favourite called *la grise* (the gray). Over several nights, Léveillé, who was a remarkable mimic, crept outside the window of his master's bedroom, and howled like a cat, thus keeping his employers awake. The mistress eventually commanded the apprentices to get rid of these awful (imaginary) cats, although warning them to avoid harming *la grise*, her pet. The apprentices set to work killing cats, every one that they could find in the neighbourhood – but began with *la grise*, hiding its body. The rest they slaughtered openly, knocking them unconscious and then sentencing them to death as part of a mock trial. They even provided the cats with a confessor before executing them! The mistress reappeared, and was convinced – but could not prove – that they had murdered *la grise*. The master turned up, and berated them for enjoying themselves killing cats rather than getting on with their work. And the apprentices laughed and laughed. 'Printers know how to laugh', Contat writes; 'it is their sole occupation'.

Contat makes it clear in his narrative that killing the cats was a way of getting at the master, and that the life of a printer's apprentice was not a very happy one. He contrasts the opulence of his employer's lifestyle with his own miserable state. Keeping cats as pets (and caring for them better than the apprentices) serves as an image to emphasize the self-indulgence of the *bourgeois* master, and his distance from the lives of his workers. But this does not really explain the wholesale slaughter, or the laughter (which occurs not only after the bloody deed, but during it too). To do that, as Darnton points out, we need to examine the varied symbolism of cats in the eighteenth century. They were still associated with witchcraft and bad luck. They were also connected to the upper orders of society – not only through their indulgence as pets, but also through folktales such as 'Puss in Boots', and perhaps because of their natural air of indolence. Torturing cats was common in several strands of European culture, as part of rituals of license and disorder. And cats were associated with women and with sex; *la chatte* having the double meaning of 'pussy' in modern English. Contat's massacre of cats made *sense* to an eighteenth-century Frenchman in a way in which we no longer respond ourselves. The apprentices, Contat tells us, would re-enact the massacre in mime on many future occasions, satirizing the reactions of the master and mistress for the amusement of their fellows. The laughter of the apprentices – for it is more a tale about humour than about cats – can be seen as part of an early-modern tradition of rebellion through mockery, a linking of riotous behaviour and humour.

We might then posit a particular 'eighteenth-century way of thinking' which associated cats with privilege, and the killing of cats with rebellion. We might also (as Darnton suggests) see links between a 'way of thinking' which delighted in slaughtering cats at a mock court with later events in eighteenth-century France. During the French Revolution, for example, the rudimentary trials and subsequent massacres of more than a thousand 'counter-revolutionary' prisoners in September 1792 by the *sans-culottes* (literally 'those without britches', but figuratively 'the have-nots'). This is not to argue that the killing of cats was a practice for the killing of men, but to suggest that there can be symbolic patterns to people's actions. The idea of there being different 'ways of thinking' in the past has had a number of labels: the 'spirit of an age' or *zeitgeist*; 'cultural consciousness'; the *mentalité* (or 'mentality') of a particular time.

It is this last term which has become most common. *Mentalité* was used originally in the first half of the twentieth century by Lucien Febvre, a French historian who started, with his friend Marc Bloch, a new kind of history known as the '*Annaliste*' approach (named after the journal they founded, called *Annales*). The Annales school had several aims. One was to shift the study of history away from political events (effecting another escape from Thucydides' tower) to questions of economy, society, and culture. Another was to try to examine much broader sweeps of history – what they called the *longue durée* (long term) – and search for deep-rooted currents in the past. Linked to this was a desire to include a knowledge of climatic change, geographical location, and lengthy economic shifts in their understanding of historical causation. This project reached its culmination in Fernand Braudel's *The*

Mediterranean, a massive book which attempts to discuss that huge geographical area over several centuries, shifting the focus of enquiry from kings and governments to the land, the people, and the sea. The *Annales* school drastically changed the shape of historiography on the continent, although the adoption of its broader aims has been less apparent in Anglo-American history. But the notion of *mentalité* has been hugely influential on all modern historians.

Thinking about *mentalité* arose as a way of trying to get away from the 'common-sense' approach of political history, which assumed that kings, counsellors, and governors made decisions on the same 'rational' basis as the historian (and thus allowed the political historian to judge the king as 'bad' or 'weak' when they failed to make the 'right' decisions); but also as an attempt to explain elements within the sources they examined which simply did not seem to fit with contemporary ideas of what was normal. Marc Bloch, for example, analysed the phenomenon of the 'King's Touch' – the putative ability of medieval monarchs to cure diseases through physical contact. He argued that this kind of action could not be discarded as a historical curiosity, unconnected to the serious business of government, but was an integral part of royal authority – and therefore alerts us to how very *different* medieval notions of power were from our own. Emmanuel Le Roy Ladurie (another *Annaliste* historian) used inquisition records, similar to those we met in the first chapter, to chart the *mentalité* of peasants: their beliefs on magic, ritual, friendship, family, and sex. *Mentalité* is born, therefore, from a sense that the past is very different from the present; and from trying to find a way of analysing those differences, rather than laughing at them.

What the *Annales* school drew upon, and what later historians have continued to utilize, were the insights of a different discipline: anthropology. Historians interested in society and culture find that they need a way of thinking about the patterns of human interaction, the *unstated* (and sometimes unrecognized) reasons why people do the things that they do. Anthropologists, who have spent their time studying and analysing other cultures, have provided useful frameworks for thinking these things through, giving historians a language for discussing ritual, the arrangement of social space, the conduct of one gender to another, and so on. *Mentalité* has become a shorthand term for summing up all of the various assumptions, practices, and rituals found in past eras.

Using the term *mentalité* involves, as I have suggested, seeing people in the past as essentially different from our own time. We shall return later to the question of whether or not this insight is correct. We should note first of all that the idea of *mentalité* also involves two other cognitive operations: dividing the span of human history into periods; and reading historical evidence in ways never intended by its creators.

As we have seen, the impossible vastness of time has, at least since the Christian era, been divided up into more manageable proportions, such as Augustine's Six Ages of Man. The broadest and most common division is that of Antiquity, Medieval (or Middle Ages), and Modern (allowing also for the nuances of late Antiquity; early, high, and late Medieval; and early Modern). An obvious but essential point: these are divisions made by human beings, and are therefore arbitrary. People living in the 'early middle ages' would not – *could not* – have given that label to themselves. As far as they were concerned, they were living in 'now', just like us. They might have had different ideas about where their 'now' was going – that it was the last step on the journey to the end of the world and God's judgement – but it was still 'now'. We look back and carve out arbitrary lines in the sand, slicing off that period from this one, cutting over two thousand years of complexity into shapes more easily digestible. I have already mentioned the large slices: Ancient, Medieval and Modern. But there are smaller slices too, which we are wont to forget: centuries and decades for example. The 'eighteenth century' is a quick way of referring to the years 1700–1799, but it is an arbitrary division nonetheless. The modern, Western calendar has only been in operation for a few hundred years, and is culturally specific (it does not, for example, follow the same years as the Jewish or Chinese calendars). Thinking in 'centuries' as opposed to, say, 'kings' reigns' has only been common in the last two hundred years or so. When Thucydides wrote his history of the Peloponnesian war, he was hampered in producing a clear chronology for his readers by the fact that different Greek cities dated their years idiosyncratically, and even had different names for the months of the year. He had to invent his own system (he numbered the years of the war one to six, and divided them into 'winter' and 'summer') whereas we have inherited our own – similarly invented – scheme.

But these lines in the sand come to have wider associations: if we want to talk about an 'eighteenth-century way of thinking', do we suppose that this changed into something else on the midnight of 31st December 1799? We talk in the West of 'the Sixties' and 'the Seventies' to indicate something we feel to be essential or particular about those decades. But again this is shorthand – and recently modern historians have started to argue that 'the Sixties' (by which they mean a set of cultural ideas and values) *really* ran from about 1964 to 1974. Similarly, other historians sometimes discuss 'the *long* eighteenth century'; that is, a century that somehow extends beyond the hundred years usually expected. This process of carving time into periods is undoubtedly useful, and perhaps unavoidable, but one needs to be wary of it. Did everyone in 'the Sixties' wear flowers in their hair, get stoned, and go to Woodstock? Did even *most* of the people do those things? If not, why do we choose this mode of life – this *mentalité* – as the 'key' image for that decade?

Recently, there was concern in much of the developed world about possible disasters occurring in the year 2000, because it marks a millennium. Some of these worries are extreme, such as those of the 'Heaven's Gate' cult members who chose to commit suicide in the United States, believing that God's judgement was nigh. Others are seen as fairly rational, such as concerns about computer chips failing because of an inability to cope with the new date. We might, however, remember that people living before the year 1000 also experienced a degree of worry – probably more so, in fact, given that a belief in God's plan to draw human history to a close was rather more firmly held in those days. And we could also contemplate the fact that 'the year 2000' (microchip design faults notwithstanding) is a human invention, based on an arbitrary calendar only recently brought into use by one part of the world's population. What is it, exactly, that we think alters within ourselves when the year changes from '99' to '00'?

This does not mean, however, that the arbitrary division of time into periods is irrelevant to human life and history. Although the date of the millennium is arbitrary, it has undeniably affected how people behave. It has been talked about in detail on radio, television, and the Internet. It leads different people to hoard food, or to find a god, or to lose their faith, or to get very drunk, or to conceive children. It has been on our minds – part of our *mentalité*, perhaps. But it presumably will not be on the minds of people at the end of the twenty-first century, or at least will not be thought about in quite the same way. Similarly, people in the eighteenth century *did* think (and therefore act) differently from ourselves, on certain topics at least. Periodization – the division of time into smaller units – may lure us into false patterns of thought, but it is perhaps unavoidable as a way of viewing the past, and may help us to capture something of how people change over time.

To get at different ways of thinking, different *mentalités*, requires a careful use of source material. It may demand, as I have suggested, reading the material in a way in which its creators never intended, for meanings they never considered. This is often called 'reading against the grain' by modern historians; 'the grain' being the direction and argument the source *wants* to take. It should be fairly obvious that for an historian to read certain sources necessarily involves using them in a different way from their creators. For example, when fifteenth-century

Florentine officials created a massive tax record, called the *catasto*, their purpose was the financial government of their city. Modern historians have, however, taken this vast source and entered its information onto a computer database. This allowed them to see patterns in the evidence that the Florentines could never have spotted (having neither the interest nor the time): patterns of marriage, life cycle, family, gender, and the division of labour.

But other sources may be more problematic. Take, for example, John of Salisbury's *Policraticus*, a book of political philosophy written in the twelfth century. The idea of the *Policraticus* was to provide a model for royal government, and (unlike tax records) it was designed to be read by other people, not only from the author's time but in later years also. Historians can, however, read the *Policraticus* in a different way: noting John of Salisbury's use of 'the body' as an image of society (the King as the head, his counsellors as the heart, peasants as the feet and so on), they can argue that the symbol tries to provide a 'natural' and static image of medieval society, and can link this to other, frequent, uses of 'body' images in medieval culture, perhaps thus identifying a medieval *mentalité*. John of Salisbury did not 'know' that he was writing about symbolic bodies – he thought he was writing about politics. But historians can find other meanings in his text. Does this give us pause for doubt? How would we feel if some later impertinent scholar read our letters, our diaries, our emails, and argued that we did not 'know' what we were revealing when we wrote?

We might feel indignant (though, of course, we would also be dead). But one should note that whether we like it or not, texts have lives that continue to change and alter *after* the death of the author, whether or not historians get involved. The *Policraticus*, for example, was read by later writers of political theory, and they used it in rather different ways, taking other meanings from it. At a certain point it became not a model for good government, but an interesting anachronism from a past age, which allowed more 'modern' thinkers to provide better models. This

process of texts changing in meaning is not confined to learned books:
you may have heard the American songwriter Bruce Springsteen's track
Born in the USA. This was written as a protest song, about the after-
effects of the Vietnam War on American servicemen, and the way in
which their society had failed them. It was, however, quickly
appropriated as an anthem of patriotic pride by the right-wing Reagan
administration. This is the way of things: write, sing, say *anything* and it
can come to mean something different. It might also tell the audience
something about the author, of which the author is not fully aware. This
book, as much as any other, may well display my unconscious
prejudices, and perhaps those of my generation. Why have I chosen the
particular historical examples I have used in these chapters? Obviously
because I thought they were interesting, and worth thinking about; but
they were *my* choices, made at a particular moment in time, within a
particular cultural context.

Reading sources 'against the grain' is, then, not only permissible but
probably essential, if we wish to get at not only 'what' people thought,
but also *how* they did their thinking. The language and images and
symbols found in documents have become of increasing interest to
historians in the last two decades, in part because of the influence of
literary theorists on the historical profession. Words used as insults, in
different times and places, can for example show fascinating changes in
culture: in the Middle Ages you might be called a 'dog' or a 'goat'; in the
early modern period, one is more likely a 'jade' or 'rogue'. The former
comes from the rural context, and the symbolism of animals; the latter,
from ideas about sexual and social honour. But there is another problem
here, again one of language. When the historian comes to write his or
her true story, how does he or she translate a past *mentalité* for a
modern audience? Whose words do you use to explain the source (and
therefore the past): those of the dead, or those of the living?

The words of the dead can be tricky. Sometimes they are the same as,
or similar to, our words, but mean different things: 'farm', for example,

meant a rent or tax for medieval people, and in the early modern period 'lewd' (or 'lewed') indicated a lack, not of civility, but of learning. A similar problem will presumably affect later historians when they look back at the 1980s and discover various things contrarily described as 'bad' or 'wicked'. Contat's apprentices describe their master as 'bourgeois', but this pre-dated and was not the same as Karl Marx's more familiar use of the term.

Furthermore, to describe something 'as people in the past would have understood it' really means to describe events as *particular* historical people understood them, or wished them to be understood. The medieval chroniclers who recorded the English uprising of 1381 describe a mindless revolt by people acting like 'animals' – but this is not how the rebels saw matters (they thought they were acting as good English subjects, appealing to the king). Contemporary English reports of the French Revolution depict a similarly barbarous picture of the *sans-culottes*, afraid that 'the mob' might also rise up on their side of the Channel; again, however, the Revolutionaries thought they were fighting for liberty, equality, fraternity.

The historian needs to be aware of the nuances of past language – understanding, for example, the changing focus and sense of a tricky word such as 'rights' in different times and places – but must not become a slave to archaic vocabulary. 'Democracy' was born in ancient Athens, or so we like to believe; but no historian of antiquity would equate the government of that city with twentieth-century representative politics. The founders of the American Constitution spoke of 'rights' in universal and 'natural' terms ('We hold these truths to be self-evident . . .'), but they did not believe that women or the poor should have the vote, and they owned slaves. They were not complete hypocrites, but partly products of their time, and of what they took for granted in their world. It is, however, much easier to take something for granted – such as slavery – if it benefits you personally. Indeed not every eighteenth-century American supported slavery, and some political radicals were extremely critical of the practice. The words of the time are, once again, the words of *particular* groups of people, and are thus implicated in struggles of power.

The words of the living can also, however, cause us problems. Using modern labels to describe the past can be dangerously anachronistic, particularly if those labels refer to concepts which, although recently invented, lay claim to universal applicability across time and culture. Describing Renaissance Italian city-states as 'democratic', because they allowed certain citizens to elect particular officials, is to apply very modern associations of what is right and just – two other troublesome words – to a distant situation. Contemporaries would have talked of 'the common good', of 'good government', having their own models of how things were best run. Other words can be much more tricky: 'to fall in love' with someone perhaps carries, for us, images of shooting stars, soul-mates, eyes meeting, hearts beating as one. This notion of 'love' was an invention of the nineteenth century; people 'loved' in previous times, but their ideas of what that involved and meant were different, less involved, for example, with the linking of two individuals and more aware of how different families would be drawn together by marriage. This is not to deny emotion to past people – but to allow them *their* emotions, rather than to transpose onto them our own.

Sometimes it is undeniably useful to apply particular words backwards across time, allowing the historian to sum up some process or state that was only half seen by contemporaries. The danger here, however, is when the reasons for coining a term are forgotten, and repeated usage hardens it into something taken for granted and unexamined. Historical periods and events are particularly prone to this process: 'the Renaissance' and 'the Enlightenment', for example, can gain a false coherence and solidity through the familiarity of their use. Even something as prosaic as 'the English Civil War' causes problems: some historians argue that other terms, such as 'Revolt' or 'Revolution' would serve better (and mean something rather different). And, in any case, there was not one single war, but rather a series of conflicts – at least three English civil wars during the course of the seventeenth century. Another example of a tricky word is the term 'feudalism', used to describe the medieval social hierarchy of people bound by a combination of land-holding and accompanying duties. This word was a much later invention, and as various people have argued, it obscures the various arcane and disparate combinations of land-duties, wages, customs, and laws found in the Middle Ages. Nonetheless, it continues to be used; perhaps, simply, because it is a useful shorthand.

This returns us to the idea of *mentalité*, which is a shorthand for something about the culture of an age and how it affects people's thoughts and actions. I suggested above that one thing that divides historians is whether they believe people in the past were essentially the same as us, or essentially different. There is perhaps a further question: whether, when using a term like *mentalité*, a historian thinks that there is a unitary pattern to the thoughts of a particular period; whether people in, say, the sixteenth century are different from us, but different from us *in the same way*. To talk of a 'sixteenth-century way of thinking' or a 'sixteenth-century *mentalité*' can be to suggest that there is an essence of 'sixteenth-century-ness', a key or core which the historian can identify. If there *is*, this leads to a further question: if they are so different from us, how is the historian able to understand them at all?

It has been suggested that despite changes over time, there are certain things which all human beings experience throughout history, which therefore link us together: birth, sex, and death. (In fact, one could presumably also argue in this line that all human beings have experienced tiredness, headaches, and indigestion, but since these do not seem as dramatic or philosophical, we will pass over them). From these key moments of humanity, it is claimed, we can build a true understanding of past lives; stepping into their heads and thinking their thoughts once again.

The problem with this is that two of those three key moments we do not *experience* ourselves, at least not in any way we can report (I have never heard anyone describe, in convincing terms, the feeling of being born or what it is like to be dead). We have other people's experiences of observing or interacting with these moments – and here history enters once again, as these things have changed over time. Birth, for example: how women got pregnant, how they understood the process of gestation, who would be present at the birth, the rituals around birth, the treatment of new-born infants – all of these things have varied over time and place. Some ancient theories of conception maintained that only the man's seed was essential, and that the woman was simply a vessel. Certain medieval doctors thought that the woman supplied 'seed' also, and some believed that the woman had to have an orgasm in order to conceive. But, by the nineteenth century, men had somehow forgotten that women could have orgasms. Caesarian deliveries were occasionally performed in the Middle Ages, but carried with them connotations of the devil, as the child would be 'not of woman born'. Nowadays they are very common in Western societies. In the past, infants were sometimes deliberately left alone outside overnight, to see whether they were strong enough to survive (because who wants to feed an extra mouth if the child will not live very long?). In recent times, people have been arrested for leaving their children alone for less than an hour.

Death – other people's experience and understanding of death – has also varied enormously. Pre-Christian warriors hoped to meet a quick, short death, hopefully heroically in battle. Christian knights wished for long deaths, so that they would know what was coming and would have time to prepare their earthly goods and their souls. Some people used to think it was fitting and honourable to eat people as a form of burial. Some other people thought it was reasonable to lock up fellow human beings in camps in their millions and to kill them systematically. Enemies of those people thought it was a good idea to drop bombs so powerful they could kill hundreds of thousands of individuals in an instant. Some of the people who died would have thought that their souls were going to be reborn in new bodies; others thought they would live in a world beyond this world; still more thought that nothing further would happen, that death was a big full stop.

The point here is that whilst it is true that every person in every time is born and will die, their ideas about those processes vary so wildly that it is difficult to see any 'essence' there, for a historian to hang on to. Sex (which, in any case, not every person experiences, either through choice or chance) is even more chaotic. Every single period of history has had its own ideas about what combinations of age, gender, colour, position, purpose, and duration are desirable, possible, permissible, and respectable.

But so too has every human being alive today. Certainly, we tend to group together in our preferences and prejudices, and our individual imaginations are maybe not so large. But collectively we are multiple, complex, and extraordinary. I suggested at the beginning of this chapter that we, in the twentieth century, do not kill cats and find it funny. In general, of course, this is true; but it is also not the whole story. Although I've never seen it happen, I have read sufficient accounts of American teenagers torturing cats with fireworks, because they thought it funny, to suspect that this has occurred in reality. The problem – but perhaps also the solution – with *mentalité* is that the people of the past are as different from us as we are *from ourselves*. At certain moments they – and we – cohere around different patterns of behaviour, and the historian can certainly seek out those patterns; but they are neither entirely the same nor entirely different from us. Perhaps one of the things historians might do is help us to reflect on both parts of that statement, to look at the past to help us see the present anew.

This raises the question of what we think history is *for*, and why we ought to bother to do it. In the next chapter we will think some more about truth and interpretation, and why history matters.

Chapter 7
The telling of truth

On the morning of 28th May 1851, in a crowded church in Akron, a woman, an ex-slave who called herself Sojourner Truth, stood up to address the Ohio Woman's Rights Convention. There are two accounts of what Sojourner Truth said. Here (slightly edited for space) is the first:

May I say a few words? . . . I am a woman's rights. I have as much muscle as any man, and can do as much work as any man. I have plowed and reaped and husked and chopped and mowed, and can any man do more than that? I have heard much about the sexes being equal; I can carry as much as any man, and can eat as much too, if I can get it. I am as strong as any man that is now. As for intellect, all I can say is, if a woman have a pint and a man a quart – why cant she have her little pint full? You need not be afraid to give us our rights for fear we will take too much, – for we cant take more than our pint'll hold. The poor men seem to be all in confusion, and dont know what to do. . . . I have heard the bible and have learned that Eve caused man to sin. Well if a woman upset the world, do give her a chance to set it right side up again. The lady has spoken about Jesus, how he never spurned woman from him, and she was right . . . And how came Jesus into the world? Through God who created him and woman who bore him. Man, where is your part? . . . But man is in a tight place, the poor slave is on him, the woman is coming on him, and he is surely between a hawk and a buzzard.

and here (also edited) is the second:

> Well, chillen, whar dar's so much racket dar must be som'ting out
> o'kilter. I tink dat, 'twixt the niggers of de South and de women at de
> Norf, all a-talking 'bout rights, de white men will be in a fix pretty soon.
> . . . And ar'n't I a woman? Look at me. Look at my arm . . . I have plowed
> and planted and gathered into barns, and no man could head me – and
> ar'n't I a woman? I could work as much and eat as much as a man,
> (when I could get it), and bear de lash as well – and ar'n't I a woman? I
> have borne thirteen chillen, and seen 'em mos' all sold off into slavery,
> and when I cried out with a mother's grief, none but Jesus heard – and
> ar'n't I a woman? When dey talks 'bout dis ting in de head [intellect],
> what's dat got to do with woman's rights or nigger's rights? If my cup
> won't hold but a pint and yourn holds a quart, wouldn't ye be mean not
> to let me have my little half-measure full? . . . Den dat little man in black
> dar [a minister], he say woman can't have as much right as man 'cause
> Christ wa'n't a woman. *Whar did your Christ come from?* . . . From God
> and a woman. Man had noting to do with him.

The first account was written by Marius Robinson, a white man who
edited the Salem *Anti-Slavery Bugle*. He published his version in that
newspaper in June 1851. The second account was published in another
paper, the New York *Independent*, in April 1863. It was written by a white
feminist writer, Frances Dana Gage. The two versions also present
different audiences for Truth's speech. Robinson (and indeed other
sources) indicates a meeting of people who supported the call for
women's rights, and who listened respectfully. Gage tells of a hostile
crowd, of pompous men and timid women, including some who did not
want questions of slavery and race to be combined with calls for
women's rights. So which account is the truth?

We still have some other questions lingering from the previous
chapters: whether historians can understand and gain access to past
lives; whether the tales they write are '*true* stories'; and what the point

of history might be. I think we can make good on those promises, before this short book closes; and I think we can start by trying to answer the question above.

Sojourner Truth was born Isabella Van Wagenen in about 1797, in Ulster County, New York. She was the child of slaves, owned by a colonel who had fought in the American Revolution. By the age of about 30 she was a free woman, although her children remained enslaved. She was devoutly religious, illiterate, and obviously possessed of a powerful character. She adopted her new and resonant name in 1843, became involved in the abolitionist movement, the American Civil War, and the fight for women's rights. Details of her life are found in the *Narrative of Sojourner Truth*, an autobiography she dictated and published in several versions. She became a woman of some fame during her life (meeting three different American presidents), and has become a symbol of African-American resistance and feminist protest, remembered chiefly now for the 'Ar'n't I a woman?' speech.

We have other accounts of the lives of slaves and ex-slaves from the nineteenth century, many written or dictated by the people themselves. One might then try to reconstruct a *mentalité* for black Americans at that time, a mode of shared thought and language, and thus decide which account of the speech at Akron fits better within this model. This might lead us towards preferring Gage's account: it is written in dialect (for surely an illiterate black woman would not speak the accurate English of the first account?), it shows what might be an 'authentic' lack of familiarity with abstract concepts such as 'intellect', and it resounds with a poetic ring of oral performance ('Ar'n't I a woman?') that connects with black American traditions of religious preaching.

But the problem with *mentalité* as a concept is that it can flatten out all difference, mould the complexity of human idiosyncrasy into *one* picture of what is 'normal' for a time and place. And these elements of 'normality' are necessarily drawn from sources, usually written

I SELL THE SHADOW TO SUPPORT THE
SUBSTANCE.
SOJOURNER TRUTH.

19. Sojourner Truth

documents, which are themselves *representations* of how people spoke, thought, and behaved. The historian Nell Irvin Painter, biographer of Sojourner Truth, tells us that Truth did not, in general, like having her words reported in dialect. Whereas we might see the phonetic spelling as representing authenticity, Truth suspected it belittled the meaning of what she had to say. To decide that the second account of the Akron speech is true, because it looks more like the words we would expect from an uneducated black woman, is to dissolve the individual Sojourner Truth into a melting pot of 'black woman-ness' – and to fail to ask ourselves how we have come by our expectations. This is not to say that one cannot attempt a more nuanced and subtle reconstruction of *mentalité*, but the dangers of assuming that there is *one* mode of thought remain. *Mentalité* may obscure variation and difference; it can also hide the existence of struggle and conflict. Sojourner Truth was engaged in just such a struggle: at heart, to get white men to think *differently* about gender and about race.

In trying to decide which account is true, but also to understand Sojourner Truth as a historical actor, the historian might be seen as caught between two roles. On the one hand, the imaginative recreator of past events: asking him or herself 'if *I* had been in that church, what would I have heard said? What would it have meant to me?' On the other, the hardened detective, demanding of the sources 'which one of you is lying to me?' Anglo-American historians have been fond of depicting this dichotomy as a conflict between History as Art and History as Science, asking within which camp our subject truly belongs. But this is, and always has been, a silly question, that wilfully misunderstands the nature of both art and science, pretending that the latter involves no imagination or insight, and that the former contains no close observation or methodical craft. It also polarizes two kinds of knowledge: a truth that is grounded in meaning and perception, and a truth that is based on inert fact and prosaic 'reality'. Put another way, it is to ask the age-old question of whether historical knowledge is subjective (dependent on the observer) or objective (independent of the observer).

If we took up the 'detective' position, we would probably decide that the first account of the Akron speech is true. It was written very close to the time of the event, the writer knew Sojourner Truth well, and had an ear for language, such that (as Painter argues) he was unlikely to have missed a fourfold refrain of that beautiful phrase 'Ar'n't I a woman?' Robinson's is the account that most historians now accept as the truth, following this kind of careful analysis of the evidence.

However, the image of the historian as detective (so beloved by generations of writers) omits the final chapter of the crime story: the courtroom scene. Whilst the detective attempts to decide which account is right and which is wrong, the tale is only done when the jury has delivered its verdict. For the audience to the battle of truth and falsehood must also decide the *import* of the conflicting stories. And in history, unlike in law, the same case can be re-tried many times. This is to suggest two things: first, that the polarity of fact and meaning is untenable, as no 'fact', no 'truth', can be spoken outside a context of meaning, interpretation and judgement. Secondly, that truth is therefore a process of *consensus*, as what operates as 'the truth' (what gets accepted as 'the *true* story') relies on a general, if not absolute, acceptance by one's fellow human beings.

It is likely that Robinson's account of Sojourner Truth's words is more accurate than Gage's poetic version. But Gage's retelling may capture something different about that woman, how she acted and was perceived by those who knew her. Finally, however, *we do not know*. The historian can imagine him or herself back in that church, and can try to examine the sources with all necessary diligence, care, and open-minded sympathy. But he or she cannot actually *be* there. And if he or she could, there is no guarantee that what the historian heard issue from Truth's lips would match exactly what every other soul in that audience thought they heard. As every detective and historian knows, accounts that match exactly usually indicate collaboration in composition rather than independent reporting. Robinson's and Gage's accounts correspond on most of the matters that Truth spoke about, although they differ in order of topic and the words used. So what we are struggling with here is a matter of feeling and meaning.

To decide 'which version is True' is also to turn one version into detritus, something to be discarded. But do we want to discard something as beautiful as 'Ar'n't I a woman'? This is not to suggest that historians should not aim at truth, for, if nothing else, *true* stories are more likely to persuade the jury to consensus. But it is to argue that if we ask for one, sole, monolithic Truth, we may silence other possible voices, different histories.

This is more than a romantic caveat, for the process of silencing other historical stories has been predominant for more than two thousand years. Thucydides' tower of political history shut out the sound of other voices, other pasts, although (as we have seen) there have been partial escapes from those walls at various times. The tower only fell, however, in the twentieth century, and fell most completely in the last thirty years. Political history and the narrative of events now take their respected places alongside *other* true stories, the stories of the vast majority of the people from all times, places, and cultures. Social history has been transformed from 'history . . . with the politics taken out' (as the British historian G. M. Trevelyan once described it) to a lively, argumentative and powerful field, combining the insights of Marxism, anthropology, sociology, and annaliste *mentalité* to produce an understanding of the everyday lives of past peoples, and how these lives combine to affect 'what really happened'. It should be clear by now that the actions of the general populace have just as much to do with 'big' events as decisions made by a small group of elite kings, politicians, and rulers: without the George Burdetts, there would be no colonization of

America; without the *sans-culottes*, no French Revolution; without the Sojourner Truths, no abolition of slavery.

But social history has also given birth to further questions. In the post-war period, feminist historians began to question whether women were satisfactorily contained within the term '*man*kind', and to investigate whether women might be said to have had their *own* history. Studies of the position of women in the middle ages and the early modern period chart a rather different story of struggle from the progressive narrative of men's affairs. Women in the late fourteenth century, for example, almost certainly had more choices, freedoms, and economic independence than their sisters in the late fifteenth century. The project of women's history, which originally aimed to recover the voices of those originally 'hidden from history', has in recent years also led to new questions about the relationships between the sexes, the patterns to which gender conforms in different periods, and the ways in which these things affect other areas of life and politics. The manner in which one is expected to 'be' a woman, and indeed to 'be' a man, has changed across time, and has informed other patterns of behaviour, from the ways in which Queen Elizabeth I of England controlled her realm, to the training in the English public schools of muscular Christian chaps who would form an officer class in the First World War.

Black historians, particularly in the United States, have engaged in their own recovery of voices hidden in the past, finding that there is a wealth of evidence not only for the conduct of slavery from the masters' viewpoint, but also the songs, accounts, and autobiographies of black people (not all, in any case, slaves) themselves. As with gender, 'race' – as a way of thinking and looking – has become a productive category for investigation, to see how people have understood and legitimized their subjection of other people, and how those thus enslaved or colonized have negotiated the experience. These histories have sought to challenge the monotone voice of traditional history, not only to find a place for other viewpoints and other stories, but also to make historians realize how much they unthinkingly take for granted. Since historians tend to pride themselves on their ability to question *everything*, this can only be a good thing. The most recent example has been those historians who have investigated the histories of gay and lesbian people. Apart from the importance of finding that such people did indeed exist in the past (one can find, for example, the interrogation of a gay man in a medieval inquisition register), an investigation of people's sexual identities and behaviours across time also challenges a lot of contemporary assumptions about what is 'normal' and 'natural'. The ancient Greeks, to pick an obvious example, did not appear to see men-having-sex-with-men, and men-having-sex-with-women, as two opposite and polarized kinds of behaviour. The terms 'homosexual' and 'heterosexual' (and, for that matter, 'gay' and 'straight') would have made no sense to them.

To return to the question of Truth, by way of these thoughts, the danger in deciding in favour of one account against another is that it aims to mould 'history' into a *single* true story. This is the logic too of seeking an 'objective' or 'scientific' history – neither of which is possible, in the way that they're meant to be. Both are attempts by subjective historians (with their own prejudices, class interests, sexual politics) to present *their* version of events as the only possible version. But the idea of a single true story – of History, with a capital H – remains tremendously attractive, and hence tremendously dangerous. Newspapers talk daily of how 'History' will judge politicians or events; politicians argue for foreign policy on the basis of 'what History shows us'; warring factions across the globe justify their killing on the basis of 'their History'. This is History with the people left out – for whatever has happened in the past, and whatever it is made to mean in the present, depends upon human beings, their choices, judgements, actions, and ideas. To label the true stories of the past 'History' is to present them as having happened independent of human interaction and agency.

None of this, however, means that historians should abandon the 'truth' and concentrate simply on telling 'stories'. Historians must stick with what the sources make possible, and accept what they do not. They cannot invent new accounts, or suppress evidence that does not fit with their narratives. But, as we have seen, even abiding by these rules does not solve every puzzle left by the past, and cannot produce a single, uncomplicated version of events. If we can accept that 'truth' does not require a capital 'T', does not happen outside human lives and actions, we can try to present truth – or rather *truths* – in their contingent complexity. To do any less is both to let down ourselves, and the voices of the past. In telling the tale of Sojourner Truth, we may well present the reasons why Robinson's account of her Akron speech is likely to be the more accurate (explaining the processes whereby we reach that judgement); but we should also tell of Gage's version, and place both into the wider 'truth' of what the words and actions of that remarkable woman meant and came to mean. We should also point to what we do not, and cannot know: the magic of hearing Sojourner Truth's oral poetry, which can be reported but not recreated. Dead voices must be allowed to keep their silences too.

What I am suggesting here is complex, but its importance demands a careful reading. To relinquish 'Truth' and the idea of *one* history does not lead to absolute relativism, where any version of events is taken as being equally valid as any other. It does not, for example, give succour to those charlatans and ideologues who seek to deny that the Holocaust ever happened. The evidence for the systematic murder of more than six million people by the Nazis is overwhelming. To try to argue that it never occurred is to violate the voices of the past, to suppress that evidence which goes against the twisted thesis. The same is true for less fraught examples: dispensing with 'Truth' does not mean dispensing with accuracy and attention to detail, and to suggest for example that the colonization of the New World never happened would be equally untenable. So too would it be to claim that this colonization was not bought in part by the untimely deaths of colossal numbers of native Americans.

However, to argue about what the Holocaust *means* is somewhat more complex. The consensus is rightly so strong on this topic that we know the Holocaust to have been an act of astounding evil. We may well decide that it was the *most* evil act ever perpetrated by human beings on fellow people. But even when agreeing with this judgement, we should take care over whether we are preventing ourselves from asking further questions, and thus turning the Holocaust into an impassable barrier, not only for morality but also for enquiry. For example, by whom was this abomination committed? If our answer is 'Adolf Hitler', we may lose sight of those Germans, Austrians, French, Swiss, and others who actively participated or passively colluded in the crime. If we examine the anti-Semitism of Germany alone, we hide the anti-Semitic and fascist elements within other countries of the period (for example, the pre-war English fascists led by Oswald Mosley). These complexities do not diminish the horror and the atrocity of what was committed in German concentration camps – but they will hopefully lead us to a better understanding of what human beings (not monsters) were capable. A better understanding of *ourselves*.

So if history is so complex, so *difficult*, and not totally secure, why do it? Why does history matter? It is sometimes suggested that we should study history to learn lessons for the present. This strikes me as problematic. If we mean by this that history (or History) presents us with lessons to be learnt, I have yet to see any example of anyone paying attention in class. Apart from anything else, were these lessons (patterns, structures, necessary outcomes) to exist, they would allow us to predict the future. But they do not; the future remains as opaque and exciting as ever it did. If, however, we mean that the past presents us with an opportunity to *draw* lessons for consideration, I am more persuaded. Thinking about what human beings have done in the past – the bad and the good – provides us with examples through which we might contemplate our future actions, just as does the study of novels, films, and television. But to imagine that there are concrete patterns to past events, which can provide templates for our lives and decisions, is to project onto history a hope for certainty which it cannot fulfil.

Another suggestion, mentioned at the beginning of this book, is that history provides us with an identity, just as memory does for an individual. This is certainly true as a phenomenon: various groups, from Protestant Ulstermen to Inuit Indians, lay claim to past events as a basis for their collective identities. But it is also a danger, as the bloody conflicts between different ethnic groups across Europe surely attest. We can lay claim to the past for part of our identity, but to become imprisoned by the past is to lose something of our humanity, our capacity for making different choices and choosing different ways of seeing ourselves.

It is also sometimes thought that history can show us some deep, fundamental insights into the human condition; that sifting through the past we may discover some intrinsic thread to our lives. Ranke's 'only to say, how it really was' can also be translated as 'only to say how it *essentially* was'. Historians have long been charged with the job of divining 'essences', to human nature, God, situations, laws, and so on. But are 'essences' of any use to us now? Do we believe in any 'essential' links between different peoples and times? If we do, it is because we wish to present universal human rights, we wish to hang on to decency and hope. And as well we should. But the historian is not, and should not be, of much use here: the historian can remind us that 'human rights' are a historical invention (no less 'real' for all that) just as are 'natural law', 'property', 'family', and so on. 'Essences' can get us into trouble, as when we come to believe that the term 'man' can always stand in for 'woman' also; or when we think that different 'races' have intrinsic characteristics; or when we imagine that *our* mode of politics and government is the only proper pattern of behaviour. So the historian might take on another job: as reminder to those who seek 'essences' of the price that might be exacted.

I want to suggest three alternative reasons for doing history, and for why it matters. The first is simply 'enjoyment'. There is a pleasure in studying the past, just as there is in studying music or art or films or botany or the stars. Some of us gain pleasure from looking at old documents, gazing at old paintings, and seeing something of a world that is not entirely our own. I hope that if nothing else, this short introduction has allowed you to enjoy certain elements of the historical past, that you have gained pleasure in meeting Guilhem de Rodes, Lorenzo Valla, Leopold von Ranke, George Burdett, and Sojourner Truth.

Leading on from this is my second reason: using history as something with which to think. Studying history necessarily involves taking oneself out of one's present context and exploring an alternative world. This cannot help but make us more aware of our own lives and contexts. To see how differently people have behaved in the past presents us with an opportunity to think about how *we* behave, why we think in the ways we do, what things we take for granted or rely upon. To study history is to study ourselves, not because of an elusive 'human nature' to be refracted from centuries gone by, but because history throws us into stark relief. Visiting the past is something like visiting a foreign country: they do some things the same and some things differently, but above all else they make us more aware of what we call 'home'.

Lastly, my third reason. This again is connected with the first two: to think differently about oneself, to gather something of how we 'come about' as individual human beings, is also to be made aware of the possibility of doing things differently. This returns me to a point made in the first chapter of this book: that history is an argument, and arguments present the opportunity for *change*. When presented with some dogmatist claiming that 'this is the only course of action' or 'this is how things have always been', history allows us to demur, to point out that there have always been *many* courses of action, *many* ways of being. History provides us with the tools to dissent.

We must bring this short book to a close. Now that I have made the introductions ('Reader, this is history; history, this is the reader') I greatly hope you will continue your acquaintance.

There is a writer I much admire, an American novelist called Tim O'Brien. He spent time as a soldier in Vietnam, and his writing struggles with the possibility and impossibility of telling a 'true war story', and what that might mean. He captures, much better that myself, the tremendous importance of the paradox within that phrase. To him, then, we give the last words:

'But this is true too: stories can save us'.

References

Chapter 1

Douglas Adams, *Life, the Universe and Everything* (London, 1985)

Michael Clanchy, *From Memory to Written Record: England 1066–1307*, 2nd edition (Oxford, 1993).

Annette Pales-Gobilliard (ed.), *L'Inquisiteur Geoffroy d'Ablis et les Cathares du Comté de Foix (1308–1309)* (Paris, 1984).

Chapter 2

Jean Bodin, *Method for the Easy Comprehension of History* (New York, 1966).

M. H Crawford and C. R. Ligota (eds.), *Ancient History and the Antiquarian: Essays in Memory of Arnaldo Momigliano* (London, 1995).

Antonia Gransden, *Historical Writing in England c.550 to the early sixteenth century*, 2 vols. (London, 1974).

Louis Green, 'Historical Interpretation in Fourteenth-Century Florentine Chronicles', *Journal of the History of Ideas* 28 (1967).

Gerald A. Press, *The Development of the Idea of History in Antiquity* (New York, 1982).

Beatrice Reynolds, 'Shifting Currents in Historical Criticism', *Journal of the History of Ideas* 4 (1953).

Richard Southern, 'Aspects of the European Tradition of Historical Writing' I – IV, *Transactions of the Royal Historical Society*, 5th series, 20–23 (1970–1973).

William of Malmesbury, *Chronicle of the Kings of England* (London, 1866).

Chapter 3

Stefan Berger, Mark Donovan and Kevin Passmore (eds.), *Writing National Histories: Western Europe since 1800* (London, 1999).

Peter Burke, *The Renaissance Sense of the Past* (London, 1969).

Edward Gibbon, *The History of the Decline and Fall of the Roman Empire* (London, 1910).

David Hume, *Enquiries Concerning Human Understanding and Concerning the Principles of Morals* (Oxford, 1975)

G. G. Iggers and J. Powell (eds.), *Leopold von Ranke and the Shaping of the Historical Discipline* (Syracuse, NY, 1990).

Donald R. Kelley, *Foundations of Modern Historical Scholarship: Language, Law and History in the French Renaissance* (New York, 1970).

Stan A. E. Mendyk, *Speculum Britanniae; Regional Study, Antiquarianism and Science in Britain to 1700* (Toronto, 1989).

Arnaldo Momigliano, *Studies in Historiography* (London, 1966).

Peter Hans Reill, *The German Enlightenment and the Rise of Historicism* (Berkeley, 1975).

The Works of Voltaire; a contemporary version, trans. W. F. Fleming (New York, 1927).

Leopold von Ranke, *The Secret of World History: Selected Writings on the Art and Science of History*, ed. R. Wines (New York, 1981).

Hayden White, *Tropics of Discourse: Essays in Cultural Criticism* (Baltimore, 1978).

Chapter 4

Calendar of State Papers, Colonial Series 1574–1660, ed. W. Noel Sainsbury (London, 1860), vol. I.

Calendar of State Papers, Domestic Series, ed. John Bruce (London, 1858–93).

Great Yarmouth Assembly Book 1625–1642 [NRO, YC 19/6].

The Journal of John Winthrop 1630–1649, eds. R. S. Dunn, J. Savage and L. Yeandle (Cambridge, MA, 1996).

Letter of George Burdett to Archbishop Laud, December 1635 [PRO, CO1/8/88].

The New England historical and genealogical register, 1847–1994, New England Historic Genealogical Society (Boston, 1996) CD-ROM collection.

Richard Cust, 'Anti-Puritanism and Urban Politics: Charles I and Great Yarmouth', *Historical Journal* 35, 1 (1992), 1–26.

Jacques Rancière, *The Names of History* (New York, 1993).

Roger Thompson, *Mobility and Migration: East Anglian Founders of New England 1629–1640* (Cambridge, MA, 1994).

I have not dealt with all of the available evidence in this chapter: there is more colonial material on Burdett, and further details on his English court cases than I found space to discuss here, including a reference in a list of Cambridge alumni that states that he died in Ireland in 1671.

References to Chapters 5 to 7 are included within the 'Further Reading' section.

Further Reading

Chapter 1

On inquisitors and Cathars, see Malcolm Lambert, *The Cathars* (Oxford, 1999), or Michael Costen, *The Cathars and the Albigensian Crusade* (Manchester, 1997). For more details and stories about life in the Pyrenees, there is Emmanuel Le Roy Ladurie, *Montaillou; Cathars and Catholics in a French Village 1294–1324* (London, 1980). This gets it rather 'wrong' some of the time, but is nonetheless interesting and entertaining. For further thoughts on who history is 'for', see Keith Jenkins, *Re-Thinking History* (London, 1991).

Chapter 2

Herodotus, *The Histories* (Harmondsworth, 1954) is much more fun to read than Thucydides, *History of the Peloponnesian War* (Harmondsworth, 1972), although the speeches in the latter can fascinate. For more detailed accounts on the history of history, see Denys Hay, *Annalists and Historians; Western Historiography from the VIIIth to the XVIIIth Century* (London, 1977); Beryl Smalley, *Historians in the Middle Ages* (London, 1974); Alain Schnapp, *The Discovery of the Past: the Origins of Archaeology* (London, 1993); Peter Burke, *The Renaissance Sense of the Past* (London, 1969). Arnaldo Momigliano, *The Classical Foundations of Modern Historiography* (Berkeley, 1990) is a very readable argument about the relationship between ancient and modern historiography. In trying out medieval and renaissance historians, one might begin with Richard Vaughan (ed.), *The Illustrated Chronicles of Matthew Paris* (Stroud, 1993); Jean Froissart, *Chronicles* (Harmondsworth, 1968); Niccolo Machiavelli, *History of Florence* (New York, 1960).

Chapter 3

Eighteenth-century authors – Gibbon and Voltaire in particular – are still a pleasure to read. On the developments, and their contexts, addressed in this chapter, see Norman Hampson, *The Enlightenment* (London, 1968); Anthony Grafton, *The Footnote; a Curious History* (London, 1997); Roy Porter, *Edward Gibbon: Making History* (London, 1988); Peter Novick, *That Noble Dream: the 'Objectivity Question' and the American Historical Profession* (Cambridge, 1988). For one description of twentieth-century approaches to historiography, see Anna Green and Kathy Troup (eds.), *The Houses of History* (Manchester, 1999).

Chapter 4

Apart from a brief mention in the article by Cust, listed in the 'References' section, no one has as yet written in detail about Burdett. On the political context within England, one can look to John Morrill, *Revolt in the Provinces: the People of England and the Tragedies of War 1630–1648*, 2nd edition (London, 1999), and more generally see Keith Wrightson, *English Society 1530–1680* (London, 1982). On Winthrop and America, see Richard Dunn, *Puritans and Yankees: the Winthrop Dynasty of New England 1630–1717* (Princeton, 1962). For another view on sources and their uses, see John Tosh, *The Pursuit of History*, 2nd edition (London, 1991), particularly chapters 2 and 3. On how historians work, see also Ludmilla Jordanova, *History in Practice* (London, 2000). A further *activity* would be to visit your nearest record office, and have a look!

Chapter 5

For a short and clear introduction to interpretations mentioned here, see Ann Hughes, *The Causes of the English Civil War* (London, 1998), and for one viewpoint discussed in detail, David Underdown, *Revel, Riot and*

Rebellion: Popular Politics and Culture in England 1603–1660 (Oxford, 1985). On Marxism, try the very readable Karl Marx and Friedrich Engels, *The German Ideology*, ed. C. J. Arthur (London, 1974), and the essays in Eric Hobsbawm, *On History* (London, 1998). Thoughts on history's relationship with other disciplines are discussed in Peter Burke, *History and Social Theory* (Oxford, 1992) and Adrian Wilson, *Rethinking Social History: English Society 1570–1920 and its Interpretation* (Manchester, 1993), and the 'Grand Narrative' is examined in Robert F. Berkhofer, Jr., *Beyond the Great Story; History as Text and Discourse* (Cambridge, MA, 1995).

Chapter 6

On the killing of cats, and other thoughts about cultural history, see Robert Darnton, *The Great Cat Massacre and Other Episodes in French Cultural History* (London, 1984). For an influential 'Annales' text, try Marc Bloch, *The Historian's Craft* (Manchester, 1953). A recent work on *mentalité* is that of Henri Martin, *Mentalités Médiévales XIe-XVe siècle* (Paris, 1996), and a critique of the concept is found in Dominick LaCapra, *History and Criticism* (Ithaca, 1985).

Chapter 7

The texts and background to Sojourner Truth are found in Nell Irvin Painter, *Sojourner Truth: a Life, a Symbol* (New York, 1996). On how sex has altered across the ages, see Thomas Laqueur, *Making Sex: Body and Gender from the Greeks to Freud* (Cambridge, MA, 1990), which can be supplemented with Helen King, *Hippocrates' Women: Reading the Female Body in Ancient Greece* (London, 1998) and the highly enjoyable James Davidson, *Courtesans and Fishcakes: the Consuming Patterns of Classical Athens* (London, 1997). An example of thinking with history is Michel Foucault, *The History of Sexuality: Volume One* (London, 1984) which has been criticized by (whilst also influencing) the previous books – but which has a rather different *project*: trying to allow an opportunity to change the present. A different view on the purpose of history is given by Gerda Lerner, *Why History Matters* (Oxford, 1998), and various thoughts on how 'History' is used by society, for good and ill, can be found in David Lowenthal, *The Heritage Crusade* (Cambridge, 1997). Finally, our last words come from Tim O'Brien, *The Things They Carried* (London, 1990).

Index

Expand your collection of
VERY SHORT INTRODUCTIONS

Available now

1. Classics
2. Music
3. Buddhism
4. Literary Theory
5. Hinduism
6. Psychology
7. Islam
8. Politics
9. Theology
10. Archaeology
11. Judaism
12. Sociology
13. The Koran
14. The Bible
15. Social and
    Cultural Anthropology
16. History
17. Roman Britain
18. The Anglo-Saxon Age
19. Medieval Britain
20. The Tudors
21. Stuart Britain
22. Eighteenth-Century Britain
23. Nineteenth-Century Britain
24. Twentieth-Century Britain
25. Heidegger
26. Ancient Philosophy
27. Socrates
28. Marx
29. Logic
30. Descartes
31. Machiavelli
32. Aristotle
33. Hume
34. Nietzsche
35. Darwin
36. The European Union
37. Gandhi
38. Augustine
39. Intelligence
40. Jung
41. Buddha
42. Paul
43. Continental Philosophy
44. Galileo
45. Freud
46. Wittgenstein
47. Indian Philosophy

Available soon

Ancient Egypt
Animal Rights
Art Theory
The Brain
Chaos
Cosmology
Design
Drugs
Economics
Emotion
Ethics
Evolution
Evolutionary Psychology
Fascism
The Fall of the Soviet Union
The First World War
Free Will
International Relations
Mathematics
Modern Ireland
Molecules
Northern Ireland
Opera
Philosophy
Philosophy of Religion
The Russian Revolution
Terrorism
World Music

Visit the
VERY SHORT INTRODUCTIONS
Web site

www.oup.co.uk/vsi

➤ **Information** about all published titles

➤ News of **forthcoming books**

➤ **Extracts** from the books, including titles not yet published

➤ **Reviews** and views

➤ **Links** to other **web sites** and main OUP web page

➤ Information about **VSIs in translation**

➤ **Contact** the editors

➤ **Order** other **VSIs** on-line